William Horatio Barnes

The Body Politic

William Horatio Barnes

The Body Politic

ISBN/EAN: 9783337133221

Printed in Europe, USA, Canada, Australia, Japan

Cover: Foto ©Suzi / pixelio.de

More available books at **www.hansebooks.com**

The Body Politic.

BY

WILLIAM H. BARNES.

PUBLISHERS:
MOORE, WILSTACH & BALDWIN,
No. 25 WEST FOURTH STREET, CINCINNATI.
NEW YORK: 60 WALKER STREET.
1866.

Entered according to Act of Congress, in the year 1866, by
MOORE, WILSTACH & BALDWIN,
In the Clerk's Office of the District Court of the United States for the Southern District of Ohio.

CONTENTS.

	PAGE
INTRODUCTION	7

CHAPTER I.
America in Figures.. 15

CHAPTER II.
National Zoology.. 21

CHAPTER III.
National Brutality.. 27

CHAPTER IV.
National Humanity... 32

CHAPTER V.
Infancy of the Nation... 38

CHAPTER VI.
Modes of National Growth.. 46

CHAPTER VII.
Of what Substance the Body Politic Consists...... 55

CHAPTER VIII.
One Head Better than Two.. 62

CHAPTER IX.
Hardness of Bone Essential to Uprightness...... 71

CONTENTS.

CHAPTER X.
How Political Bone Becomes Compact.......... 82

CHAPTER XI.
Phosphorus in the Body—Pains and Pleasures of Fire-Eating........................... 90

CHAPTER XII.
National Nerves—Their Former and their Latter Uses.. 101

CHAPTER XIII.
Our Main Artery and its Important Functions.. 108

CHAPTER XIV.
Our Landed Estate, and how we have a Rich Uncle.. 120

CHAPTER XV.
Folly of Affection for a Part and Hatred of the Whole....................... 133

CHAPTER XVI.
How Deadly Disorder is Contracted, and Cure Accomplished by Desperate Remedy............. 139

CHAPTER XVII.
Nervousness—A Modern Malady which Befalls the Mother of First Families.................... 150

CHAPTER XVIII.
The Mind which Animates the Body Politic...... 157

CHAPTER XIX.
THE NATIONAL WILL—WHO MAY EXPRESS IT AND OF WHAT COLOR THEY MUST BE...... 165

CHAPTER XX.
LEGISLATION—HOW THE POPULAR WILL, UTTERED AT THE BALLOT-BOX, BECOMES LAW...... 177

CHAPTER XXI.
EXECUTIVE—QUALIFICATIONS REQUIRED IN THE MAN WHO CARRIES OUT NATIONAL WILL...... 197

CHAPTER XXII.
JUDICIARY—HOW WE INTERPRET OUR LAWS...... 219

CHAPTER XXIII.
FROM JERUSALEM TO JERICHO—SCENES FROM OUR QUADRENNIAL ELECTIONS....... 230

CHAPTER XXIV.
HOW THE PUBLIC MIND IS EDUCATED...... 239

CHAPTER XXV.
THE AMERICAN LANGUAGE—OUR GOOD HERITAGE AND HOW WE USE IT...... 247

CHAPTER XXVI.
PUBLIC PIETY—DIFFERENCE BETWEEN A RELIGIOUS STATE AND A STATE RELIGION...... 260

CHAPTER XXVII.
INTEMPERANCE—OUR UNPROFITABLE PARTNERSHIP... 270

CHAPTER XXVIII.
Our Fountain of Youth—How the Nation Renews her Strength 276

CHAPTER XXIX.
Nations are not Immortal, and States do sometimes Die 286

CHAPTER XXX.
The Paradise of Nations and the Political Life to Come 297

INTRODUCTION.

THE AUTHOR AND THE READER.

Will you have an Introduction ——.

"Certainly; we always look for one at the opening of a book."

Not so fast, good reader. I was going to ask if you would have an introduction to the most illustrious personage in the world.

"The President of the United States, the Queen of England, the Emperor of the French, the Czar of Russia, or ——."

Hold, good reader, you are looking in the wrong direction. The personage of whom I speak is greater than any and all of those worthies combined.

"Impossible! I have named the most distinguished monarchs of the earth."

The personage to whom I would introduce you is made up of sovereigns, and is greater than any crowned and sceptered monarch—THE AMERICAN REPUBLIC.

"What can be the constituents of such extraordinary greatness?"

Illustrious lineage, vast territorial domain, royal power, rare intelligence, pure morality, and the glory of distinguished deeds. She has been victorious over all her foes, and has lately subdued the greatest rebellion the world has ever seen. Presentation to such a personage will do you honor.

"She must be a dull and uninteresting person, since all that is known of her is contained in prosy histories and law books."

You have a wrong impression. A more interesting person does not exist.

"Whatever may be her personal character, the little I have seen of her in books has been anything but entertaining."

Because you have always contemplated the Republic in the abstract. You should contemplate her in the concrete, composed of living, moving, irrepressible Americans.

"When a child, I was much amused with a picture of a great Druidical idol, made of wicker work, in human shape, and filled with men and women clambering about in head and limbs and trunk. I might be amused with a figure of the American Republic, gotten up on the same principle, did I not suspect it of being a device to lead me unawares to mix in politics, something which I leave wholly to politicians."

Just so far do you come short of being a good citizen. It is a great mistake which some good people make, to suppose there is something polluting in politics, making it proper to leave it in the hands of politicians and demagogues. It is time that the better class of Americans should know more of government and take an active part in politics.

"You speak of a 'better class'—you then recognize the existence of an aristocracy in this country."

The only aristocracy I recognize is the great, free, good-at-heart American people, who constitute the majority, and consequently the best part of the nation. The politicians form a small, and, as things go, a powerful minority. The people, being divided and inattentive to their own interests, have been easily overcome by the politicians, who, notwithstanding their apparent differences, generally have a fair understanding among themselves. They have that proverbial "honor" which is said to exist among persons of dishonest proclivities. This minority, making up in strategy what they lack in numbers, are generally victorious. They practice a very sound principle of military art—divide the enemy and then conquer him in detail. Like the wolf, described by Watts, they know

"Unless the sheep they first divide they never can devour."

The people, in their virtue and honesty, have permitted themselves to know too little and take too small a part in politics.

"Would you have every citizen versed in the mysteries of statesmanship?"

Statesmanship is not so unmanageable a craft as many people imagine. Politicians have often come near making our gallant vessel a wreck. With a little more knowledge in the people to inspire them with self-confidence, they would take the helm into their own hands.

"What is the nature of this needful knowledge?"

They must first know themselves. The Science of Government, like charity, begins at home. The people should adopt the maxim of Thales, the philosopher, "*Know Thyself.*" The Greeks appreciated this so highly that they enrolled its author as first among their "Seven Sages."

"What bearing can self-knowledge have on the Science of Government?"

Every man being a constituent part of the State, and having a close resemblance to other men, when he thoroughly knows himself he has made important progress toward a knowledge of his neighbors and his nation.

"You mean that the citizen has as much resemblance to the nation as the famous brick had to the house of which the Roman sent it for a specimen."

The citizen is not merely one of the "lively stones" which form the fabric of American society; he is a little image of the Republic, every part of which has its counterpart in his own person.

If self-knowledge is carried on to self-conquest, not only the theoretical but the practical part of government is attained, and the citizen may be a wise ruler as well as an intelligent voter.

History is an important help to a knowledge of the American Government, since it details the aspirations and struggles of mankind toward great political ideas, never practically developed and realized until now.

All natural science may throw illustrative light upon the philosophy and workings of a form of government so admirably adapted to the nature of man and his surroundings.

The philosopher who first taught men to know themselves, was the first Grecian who knew anything of nature. Bringing his self-knowledge and his knowledge of nature into the arena of politics, he stands in history among the wisest and best of ancient rulers. He caused his astronomical knowledge to subserve a political purpose, and made all his attainments auxiliary to his success in statesmanship.

In the following pages principles in politics and government are sometimes illustrated by truths of humanity and nature. A political truth and a physical fact, placed side by side, are supposed to throw illustration upon each other. By this combination, if Perception is not quickened and Intellect enlarged, Memory is aided, and Curiosity is urged toward further and profounder inquiries.

THE BODY POLITIC.

CHAPTER I.

AMERICA IN FIGURES.

MANY people are fond of figures. Some have a taste for mathematical figures, and delight in developing the properties and powers of numbers. They take pleasure in mustering the Arabic hosts which spring into existence at the touch of the magic pencil.

They have a pleasant theory that "figures do not lie," while unhappy experience has created in their minds a conjecture, amounting almost to conviction, that members of the human species sometimes prevaricate.

Patriots, with such tastes, delight to contemplate the greatness of their country, as illustrated and described by numerical figures. The ponderous volumes of the decennial census are to them more attractive works than books of poetry and romance. The transcript of a page from the census report has more thrilling interest to them than a quotation from Milton or Shakspeare. It gives the same charm to the page that pictures give to books intended to amuse or educate the young. As an illustration, pleasing to persons fond of figures, and instructive to such as have not read the Census of 1860, we present the following carefully prepared and reliable

PICTURE OF OUR POPULATION—FIGURES IN WHICH THE STATES AND TERRITORIES APPEARED IN 1860:

Alabama	964,201	Ohio	2,339,511
Arkansas	435,450	Oregon	52,465
California	379,994	Pennsylvania	2,906,115
Connecticut	460,147	Rhode Island	174,620
Delaware	112,216	S. Carolina	703,708
Florida	140,425	Tennessee	1,109,801
Georgia	1,057,286	Texas	604,215
Illinois	1,711,951	Vermont	315,098
Indiana	1,350,428	Virginia	1,596,318
Iowa	674,913	Wisconsin	775,881
Kansas	107,206	Colorado	34,277
Kentucky	1,155,684		2,261
Louisiana	708,002	Dakota	2,576
Maine	628,279	Nebraska	28,841
Maryland	687,049	Nevada	6,857
Massachusetts	1,231,066		10,507
Michigan	749,113	New Mexico	83,009
Minnesota	172,123	Utah	40,273
Mississippi	791,305		426
Missouri	1,182,012	Washington	11,168
N. Hampshire	326,073	Dist. Columbia	75,080
New Jersey	672,035		
New York	3,880,735		31,443,322
N. Carolina	992,622		

The patriot of statistical tastes delights to contemplate his country as represented thus in figures of arithmetic. To him there is no dullness in the work of casting up these long columns of figures. His pride in contemplating the "result"—the "grand total," 31,443,322—bears no resemblance to that which the schoolboy has in producing an "answer" exactly corresponding with the book. His tastes have so greatly changed since the days of his pupilage, that he rejoices in the size of his "sum," and feels patriotic pride in seeing so large a number in the place of millions, where in the first census, in 1790, there stood a solitary "3."

Not satisfied with these elementary "figures," he proceeds to cipher under the highly prophetical "Rule of Progression." Eighteen Hundred and Seventy, Eighteen Hundred and Eighty, and Eighteen Hundred and Ninety, each marshals its array of augmenting figures. These years at length hide their heads, and fall back before the mightier decades which arise in the further future. Numbers increase so rapidly as, at length, to give vigorous exercise to the powers of belief. Faith would falter, were not the mind sustained by the reassuring proverb that "Figures do not lie."

A man with another style of mind has a taste

for figures of a different kind. He becomes bewildered and lost amid the numbers which describe the vast populations of the present and the future, and takes refuge among "figures of Rhetoric." Metaphor, Simile, and Hyperbole place their brilliant pictures before his imagination. He delights in the highly-colored delineations which poetry presents of his country's present and future greatness.

Simile is a favorite figure, since it abounds in "likes," and uses them lavishly as introductions to its pleasing and instructive comparisons, thus:

"America! the sound is like a sword
To smite the oppressor! Like a loving word,
To cheer the suffering people while they pray
That God would hasten on the promised day,
When earth shall be like Heaven, and men shall stand
Like brothers round an altar, hand in hand.
O! ever thus, America! be strong,
Like cataract's thunder, pour the freeman's song,
Till struggling Europe joins the glad refrain,
And startled Asia bursts the despot's chain."

Metaphor takes up the strain, and in bolder language describes America as actually possessing the attributes of the symbol employed to illustrate its character:

"Thou noblest scion of an ancient root,
Born of the forest king! spread forth!

Spread forth!
High to the stars thy tender leaflets shoot,
Deep dig their fibers round the ribs of earth,
From sea to sea; from south to icy north,
It must erelong be thine, through good or ill,
To stretch thy sinewy boughs!"

These images do not possess that life-like character which the ardent imagination desires. Something more than empty form is required; the breath of life should animate the image which typifies the Nation. Under the glowing affection of the patriot, the country assumes a living form and human proportions, and thus enlists the sympathies to a degree that could not be done by an unembodied abstraction:

Thou, O my Country, art no ancient myth,
No vague conception in the poet's brain;
No cold abstraction of the mystic's thought;
Thou art a moving, active, present life!
Thou hast a form more beautiful and fair
Than e'er before has beautified the earth;
A head thou hast to think, a heart to feel,
A hand to do thy great and glorious work!
Thou bearest in thy breast a world of hopes;
Of human sympathies thy heart is full!
Thou strewest blessings with a lavish hand
Along the upward pathway of mankind!

The Athenians personified their country as a fair and majestic female form. Phidias, the greatest sculptor of antiquity, gave visible form to the idea which existed in the minds of his countrymen, when he reared upon the Acropolis his colossal statue of Athenè, the city's tutelar divinity, constructed of ivory and gold.

The Romans had a conception of their country, which was frequently wrought by painters and sculptors, as a queenly woman, seated on a gorgeous throne, with a helmet on her head, and emblems of world-wide dominion in her hand.

Humorous caricatures sometimes make their appearance in our attempts to personify modern nations. The eccentric figures of John Bull and Brother Jonathan are easily recognized in pictorial delineations of their exploits. None fail to distinguish, at first glance, the stout, well-rounded form of John Bull, with his smooth, full face, and firmly planted foot. A smile of recognition always greets good-humored Brother Jonathan, with his frank, expressive face, his lofty hat and striped breeches, which, from his rapid growth, long since parted company with his cowhide shoes. So different do these personages appear in costume and proportions, that nothing less than the indubitable evidence of history would induce us to suspect their relationship.

CHAPTER II.

National Zoology.

In the cumbersome alphabets of ancient times, the roughly drawn figures of animals were used as hieroglyphic symbols. Since abstract qualities could not be literally pictured to the eye, they were typified by the forms of the animals that were supposed to possess them. The fox became the emblem of cunning, the owl of wisdom, and the lion of courage.

There is a system of hieroglyphics still in universal use. Nations delight to display themselves in animal imagery. They select certain of the nobler birds and quadrupeds as symbols of their favorite attributes.

The eagle has been honored above all birds, in being most frequently chosen as a national representative. In many nations he has been elevated to this position by unanimous suffrage. He has fulfilled the duties of his office to universal satisfaction. He has not shared the fate of other office-holders. No partisan press has hurled anathemas against him, or held up his private and public life to the contempt of mankind.

Although the office is elective, it has been kept in the aquiline family, and handed down from one generation to another, as a kind of hereditary right.

The Tuscans sought on one occasion to confer a compliment on the young and sturdy State of Rome, whose friendship, they presumed, might some day grow to be of value. They cast about to devise some delicate and sentimental mode of bestowing flattering attention. They could think of nothing more suitable than an ivory eagle, standing on a scepter, leaving the interpretation of the symbol to the discernment of the Roman people. They would have shown themselves exceedingly obtuse, and anomalous among men, if they had been unable to comprehend a compliment. With a facility always characteristic of the Roman people, in appropriating to themselves whatever would augment their grandeur, they adopted the eagle as the standard of the Republic. At first it was roughly carved in wood; afterward it was made of silver, and held in its talons golden thunderbolts. At length it became a golden eagle, and thus was borne before the conquering legions of the Empire.

When all the Roman standard-bearers had fallen before their enemies, or fled from the field of battle, their ornithological symbol was seized by other nations. None, however, have borne it so worthily as America. Never has "the proud bird of our country" come to dishonor.

The American eagle differs little from that of Rome, being but a different species of the same pugnacious and aspiring family. While the Roman eagle sat calmly on the staff, in the thickest of the battle, as if noting the progress of the strife, ours displays a more uneasy and restless spirit. His wings are expanded, and he bends with protecting solicitude over a shield, whereon are painted stripes and stars. In his talons, he bears a bundle of commingled thunderbolts and arrows, wherewith, on provocation, he may vindicate his warlike prowess. This bird has not forgotten its Roman extraction, nor the language in which its ancestors used to hear the commands of imperial officers, for it bears in its beak a motto, in the Latin tongue, "*E pluribus Unum.*"

Great Britain's representative in the Natural History of Nations is the Lion—the animal described to our youthful fancy as "King of Beasts"—whose roar startles the wilderness like thunder; of whose lordly attributes all animals stand in awe; whose bones are of texture so compact as to strike fire with steel; whose muscles are like iron bands.

Of great daring and spirit must be the nation claiming such an animal as a correct embodiment of its power and disposition. Did a pusillanimous people adopt such an emblem, they would gain the contempt of other nations, and re-enact the celebrated Æsopean scene of the ass in lion's skin.

Great Britain has never been guilty of conduct inconsistent with the character of this royal beast. On many memorable occasions, the British Lion has broken from his cage and carried dismay to other beasts in the menagerie of nations. Americans, however, are by no means unanimous in the opinion that the British Lion is unconquerable. Fourth of July orators describe two occasions of his discomfiture, when "The American Eagle drove back the British Lion to his lair."

Chanticleer, songful bird of the morning, and bloody champion of barn-yard battles, is the adopted fowl of France. With haughty mien he walks at the head of the feathered inhabitants of the farm, and woe to the unhappy rival that dares to dispute his sway.

The Gallic Cock is the most pugnacious of his race. He is so fond of fighting that he never allows himself to lose an opportunity of displaying his belligerent abilities. Whether led forth to the arena by a Bonaparte or a Bourbon, he is the same spirited, plucky and pugnacious fowl. His shrill clarion has often summoned nations to the field of combat, whereon has been decided the momentous question of relative elevation upon the dung-hill of national grandeur. No reverses avail to put an end to his pertinacity. Even when he is conquered, his note sounds scarcely less loud and triumphant than the complacent crow of victory. When an adversary flies before him, no adequate idea can be conveyed of his demonstrations of satisfaction. He leaps upon the old and long-respected boundary-fence, and regales the world with martial music, expressed in his best melody and measure. He struts abroad in other inclosures, wishing to demonstrate everywhere that he is "Cock of the Walk"

James Monroe, an American of some celebrity, a few years ago built a fence which was designed to exclude all the birds and beasts of European nations from building nests or making dens in America. It was made the duty of the American Eagle to see that no unruly creature should break down or overleap this barrier. The guard having been lately called down from his lofty perch, to settle a domestic difficulty, the Gallic Cock embraced his opportunity to overleap the allotted limit, and led his feathered retinue into Mexico. Much to the distsurbance of French equanimity, our domestic troubles have come to a close, and the Gallinaceous fowl seriously contemplates a return to his ancient barn-yard. Should he manifest reluctance to go back, our redoubtable Eagle may feel called upon to lend the aid of his beak and talons.

The animal representative of Russia is the Bear, whose affectionate embrace has proven fatal to many a poor province that has fallen in his way. Seldom has the Russian Bear a season of hibernation. His vigilant eye is continually open, and his jealous heart is always astir. If another national beast gathers more spoil than himself, the congratulatory salutation which greets his ear, is an unamiable growl from the gruff Bear of Russia. He has a plantigrade step and an ungainly gait, from which the other animals find some amusement, when they are at a safe distance; but, in his presence, they are solemn and silent, out of respect for his great strength and ungraceful temper.

Napoleon Bonaparte tried the old and now unpopular amusement of Bear-baiting, but he found it an expensive and unprofitable pastime He stirred up an adversary that did not cease pursuit until he found a refuge among the rugged rocks of St. Helena.

CHAPTER III.

NATIONAL BRUTALITY.

SINCE nations have imbruted themselves and debased their natures to a level with four-footed beasts and creeping things, it is proper that they should be impersonated by animals; and be set forth as a menagerie of wild beasts for the amusement of mankind. The spectators have been greatly amused by the exhibition. When any deed of extraordinary fierceness has been performed, the applause of the multitude has made the world resound. The wise and the good, as well as the foolish and unthinking, have sometimes been carried away by the prevailing enthusiasm.

In ancient times fair and gentle ladies were wont to sit in the amphitheater of Rome, and behold with delight the bloody combats of gladiators with wild beasts. When an unusually hideous wound was inflicted, they waved their fair hands in token of unwomanly delight.

As a consequence of the diffusion of Christianity, there is less of bloodthirstiness in the masses of modern times, and yet there seems to be a great disposition to glorify the deeds of war, no matter whether performed in holy or unholy cause. The hero of a wicked faction, in an ungodly war, is lauded by men for what they are pleased to call his gallantry, when he should rather be consigned to the dungeon or the halter for his unparalleled treason, and cold-blooded murders.

While the multitude have cast garlands of flowers around the necks of the victorious beasts of war, and while the most have had eyes of admiration fixed upon the bloody monster walking in triumph, a few Florence Nightingales have bethought them of his victims, and have stolen quietly away to the bloody arena of battle to allay the fever and stanch the ghastly wounds. Alas, such ministering angels stand like bending reeds in the fiercely rushing torrent of blood.

Nations have no heart to feel, and take their chief delight in keeping open the perennial fountain of human gore. The most of that which purports to be history, is but a record of animal strength and warlike deeds. Being a narrative of deeds more appropriate to wild beasts than to men, it would be more consistently entitled Natural History, were not its incidents too revolting for the pleasing pages of a book devoted to "Animated Nature."

While nations, in preparation for their grand masquerade, have been choosing the animal masks in which they are pleased to appear, we do not wonder that the claims of some very amiable animals are overlooked. The more praiseworthy and useful the animal, the less likelihood has he of wearing the honors of national distinguishment. Other things being equal, the more useless, and even dangerous, the animal the more surely will it rise to be conspicuously paraded on a national escutcheon. Such being national taste and usage, it is easy to account for the obscurity and neglect in which certain very useful animals have lived and labored for centuries. True, the ancient Egyptians were an appreciative people, and honored the sober and useful virtues of the ox, by rendering him worship, a pitch of respect which modern nations have scarcely reached, even with the worst animals which they have selected as the objects of their admiration. It must be remarked, however, that worship with the old and thoughtless Egyptians was of little more value than a casual "Good morning!" or a "How do you do?" with us, for they performed their pious prostrations before such unworshipful weeds as leeks and onions.

The horse has been sometimes honored with a place in national heraldry, but not until he has been unharnessed from the plow, and released from the shaft of the laboring wain, and has come forth caparisoned for war, "his neck clothed with thunder, scenting the battle afar off."

It seems strange that no nation has shown so true a sense of self-appreciation as to adopt the donkey as the embodiment of national propensity. He has been long before the public, and his peculiar qualities are well known. Æsop honored him two thousand years ago, by making him the medium of communicating some of his wisest and most useful lessons. His mighty voice has enlivened every civilized land with his questionable music. His "deep-toned bass in nature's anthem" is easily recognized by all lovers of the harmony of sweet sounds, even though their "ears for music" are of proportions far inferior to those which adorn the head of his asinine highness.

Though the peculiar graces of mind and body possessed by this animal are familiar to the masses, yet his claims have never been sufficiently considered by national zoologists. His qualities are not of that showy kind which attract the attention of kings and senates. If he were possessed of claws, instead of hoofs, and carniverous teeth instead of thistle-grinding molars, his long ears, and other odious bodily and intellectual attributes, would prove no obstacle to his wearing the honors of national distinction.

CHAPTER IV.

NATIONAL HUMANITY.

SCIENCE reveals the fact that for many centuries before man's advent, the globe was inhabited by inferior orders of creation. Long before man stood forth, the crowning work of his Creator's hand, beasts of the forests and monsters of the sea had the earth as their undisputed empire.

No intelligent creature had appeared to claim dominion over the earth and subdue its wild inhabitants. Creatures of gigantic size lay with their monstrous lengths "for many a rood" along the sea, roamed the wilderness, or wheeled their drony flights through the murky atmosphere.

Generation after generation came and went, before a spark of intellectual fire was smitten from the rugged matter which composed the earth. No sound of intelligent voice broke the silence of the wilderness; no smoke of domestic fire curled through the forest; no keel of commerce rippled the lonely river or plowed the solitary seas.

This state of things did not endure. Creation was not complete with mere animal existence.

The era of higher life arrived at length. The final act of creating power was nobler and more godlike than all that had gone before. A nobler and more beautiful form than any that had before appeared, walked under the green trees of Paradise.

A hand, guided by intellect, shaped habitations and made highways on the earth. Thought at length had its high manifestations and permanent dwelling-place in the world.

Human government has had a history analogous to that of the globe. Man's arduous and unsuccessful attempts at government, seem a re-enactment of the beastly epochs of geologic times.

We have seen how nations have taken imagery for themselves from the animal world, and how well their symbols coincide with their characters.

The human age of government is at last begun. A creation has been made which marks a new era in the social and political history of mankind. In constructing the world, God suffered many centuries to elapse after He began the work of creation, before making a creature after His own image. Thus many years came and went, and man was content with inferior forms of government. He gave them all more or less of beastly shape. At last man has constructed a government after his own likeness, one that is endowed with human attributes. It has an upright body, and clearer manifestations of intellect than any that have gone before. Having been constructed on a better model, it is nearer political perfection than any predecessor.

The American people, in the construction of their government, were not careful to follow the models of antiquity. Had they adopted any other government as their example, the body politic would inevitably have borne the "mark of the beast."

The Israelites in the wilderness had a pleasing recollection of the delightful tasks and wholesome scourgings of their amiable Egyptian masters. They had a vivid recollection also of their intellectual, and ennobling devotions, when they prostrated themselves before the sacred ox. Hence when, in the absence of Moses, they attempted to frame a theology for themselves, they had before their imagination Egypt's venerated quadruped. When they cast gold into the fire, there came forth a near resemblance to the worshipful ox of Egypt, which they called a calf. With so much indignation and contempt did Moses regard the impotent idol, that he conceived it good for nothing but to be ground to powder, and mingled as a wholesome and medicinal drink. Moses had enough knowledge of materia medica to know that such a decoction would prove a powerful purgative of folly.

The Israelites, in their experiment with the calf, have given illustration of the principle that when people yield themselves in blind obedience to the past, their theologies, their governments, or whatsoever they endeavor to construct, will simply be diminutive, and imperfect repetitions of obsolete follies.

The founders of the American government were creators, rather than imitators. By their bold reflections, and simultaneous wielding of the sword, they cut the Gordian knot by which they were tied to ancient forms and usages.

With backs forever on the past, and eyes wisely fixed upon the future, they walked forth to their great work. "With firm reliance on Almighty God," they took in their skillful hands the plastic clay. They knew themselves. They recognized manhood in humanity, and molded their materials after the pattern thereof. They so constructed the beautiful body that every member might have free use of all its powers.

The craftsmen, whose cunning hands constructed our commonwealth, were unwilling to stop short with a bodily form. A body without a soul, even had it been of human proportions, would have been little better than the groveling creations of past unskillfulness. There was no need of a new creation that the frame-work of American government should be inhabited by a living soul. Freedom granted to individual minds, and a proper care directed to their development, procured the existence of a public mind of sufficient vigor of understanding and maturity of wisdom to animate the body politic.

No magician was called upon to evoke some ghastly shadow of the past. No dead and buried majesty of antiquity was summoned from the tomb to lend the glittering phosphorescence of decay to sightless eyeballs.

No galvanic batteries of vast standing armies were constructed to create spasmodic motions of electrical force, which would be but the feeble imitations of real life.

The living and present people were thought to have surplus mind enough, after devoting all needful attention to their private ends, to animate the State with a healthy and vigorous intellect. There seemed no need of a special intellect whose only office should be to think for the nation, and spend its years in devising schemes to achieve royal renown. The carrying on of government was rightly regarded as requiring no higher thoughts than a free and intelligent people could easily conceive, if left entirely to their own resources. The crowning glory of our country is its mind, which characterizes it as the first specimen of national manhood the world has ever seen. Being the work of a finite and fallen being, and being constructed in the image of its creator, it has, of necessity, much imperfection. Nevertheless it is far superior to all "four-footed beasts and creeping things."

CHAPTER V.

Infancy of the Nation.

In ancient times nations were neglected in their childhood, and left to struggle along up through infantile feebleness, without any well-timed assistance and wholesome encouragement. There was no presentiment of future greatness, hence no careful record was made of the smart sayings and precocious deeds of early years. The moss of forgetfulness was allowed to grow over the juvenile footsteps. Origin and parentage were often utterly forgotten. The old nations were all foundlings.

The Muse of history looked with indifference upon their unpromising childhoods. After awhile the performance of remarkable exploits attracted attention, and threw luster over all preceding actions, but the forgetful Muse strove in vain to recall events of the past, which she had neglected to "make a note of." Imagination was called upon to supply a childhood, which, of course, would be made of similar web and woof to that of which later life was woven, but of far more brilliant coloring. The record of the infancy of ancient nations is made up of mythical and incredible tales.

Nations whose birth has fallen upon recent centuries have been more fortunate. Every one has had an early and egotistical opinion of present importance and prospective greatness. With a presentiment of the interest which would in future gather around their names and fortunes, they have employed historians to make a record of events as they transpired. With scrupulous exactness they have made contemporary record of the progressing life.

Many of these historians have fallen into the error of describing the acts of youthful nations in language appropriate only to the greater achievements of maturer strength. Hercules is made to kill so many Lernean Hydras and clean so many Augean stables in his childhood, that no heroic labors are left for manhood. These enthusiastic chroniclers deserve the criticism which Goldsmith made on Dr. Johnson, that in his stories he made his minnows talk like whales.

Some men are said to be so unfortunate as never to have had a childhood. They entered a dusty road in their early years, and found themselves bowed beneath a burden of premature thoughtfulness and care, when they ought to have been musical with childish laughter, skipping gaily through the meadows in search of butterflies and flowers.

A happy childhood is an indispensable preparation for a good and prosperous life. It is an exhaustless treasury, whence happiness may be drawn to solace the dark hours of the future. A parent who does not strive to surround his child with circumstances which shall be sources of pleasant memories, wrongs his offspring, and is recreant to his trust.

Nothing is so prophetic of great national importance as a genuine youthful childhood. The ancient fables say that soldiers sprang up fully armed and equipped from the dragon's teeth sown by Cadmus; and Minerva leaped full-grown and panoplied from the brain of Jove; but nations have no such abrupt maturity. Their day has a gradual dawn, their growth is slow and steady. When they have reached the meridian of greatness they can sometimes look back on centuries of infancy.

The American Nation has been blessed with a long and happy childhood. This delightful period began in 1607, in the woods which shaded the shores of the Chesapeake. The range of its rambles was wide, and very soon reached from Cape Cod to the coast of Carolina.

While the infant nation might have seemed to the casual observer to be employed in the thoughtless pursuit of temporary happiness, it was really employed in most diligent preparation for the important duties of coming ages. Before the seventeenth century had passed, the broad foundations of freedom and national unity had been laid.

The opening of the last quarter of the eighteenth century witnessed our final separation from the mother country, yet this was not an end of our national childhood. It is not consistent with popular ideas of our national longevity, to suppose that we have passed through our juvenile period and arrived at maturity. Our national childhood, begun under pleasing auspices, is still in its happy continuance. Though our nation is no longer under legal restraints, nor obligations to a mother country, yet she still wears the vivacity and verdancy of youth. She is young in heart and young in ways.

In our attempts to imitate our elders, we manifest the moods and ways of infancy. All the attainments of childhood are gained by careful attention to what others do, and diligently following example. Originality in thought and deed pertains to maturer years. To such years our country has not yet attained. Our fashions and our manners are carefully formed on Paris models. Our "lions" must pass the ordeal of European exhibition before they become "the rage" in America. A tamer of horses, or a player of chess, is unnoticed among us, until he gains a European renown. A single breath of foreign fame wafts its happy recipient to the pinnacle of American celebrity. An American book's best recommendation is its republication in England, or its translation into some obscure dialect of the continent. To say of an author that he has a "European reputation" is to give him apotheosis in America. A trip to Europe is the "royal road" to excellence, the very existence of which highway, a few centuries since, was prematurely and unadvisedly denied. Hereby education is "finished," and health restored and fortified for the remainder of life. To our distant and unpracticed eyes the old world is full of beautiful and splendid things, set up as lessons for our learning and models for our imitation. We gratulate or vilify ourselves in proportion as we approach or fall below those great examples.

After all, the ability to imitate and the capability of being molded on good models, is one of the most hopeful peculiarities of childhood. It is some assurance of future national greatness that we are capable of honestly appropriating the excellencies of other nations. When maturer wisdom shall direct us to select for imitation only what is good among foreign institutions, we shall pursue our highway to greatness without making any sidelong steps.

Children sometimes disagree concerning the ownership of toys, and strive to maintain their fancied rights in unamiable ways. America and her sister nations have been involved in numerous childish quarrels. She had a scramble with Great Britain for the largest slice of the Northwest; she wanted "Fifty-four forty," but finally sat down by the Columbia river, in pouting mood, because she got but "Forty-nine."

Those "little hands," which the didactic poet teaches, "were never made" for the discoloration of eyes, were used by her in a very unamiable way against her little sister Mexico, until she was induced, greatly against her will, to surrender Texas, New Mexico and California.

As is natural in childhood, our chief efforts have hitherto been given to the promotion of bodily and material interests. Sallust complacently said, that with himself and fellow Romans the body was servant and the mind was ruler. As a nation, we have not yet reached such elevation. Our infantile body is clamorous in the assertion of its claims. It bids mind and soul stand aside until its own demands are satisfied.

Private and personal childhood is given a human being that he may have a few leisure years in which to gather up a body from earth, air, water, or what source soever suitable material may be found. All the infantile hours are monopolized in reaching this great end of juvenile creation.

"What is the great end of creation?" the philosophers inquire, and produce many learned lucubrations in eliciting their answers. "To be happy," says one; "To do good," exclaims another; "To glorify God," responds a third. While older and wiser heads are thus occupied with logical prelections and philosophic doubts, children give practical and instinctive answers to the question as applied to them; showing plainly that they suppose their childhood was given them for three important ends: to eat, to sleep, to play. Not until the body has grown to considerable length and breadth does the mind dare to make any confident assertion of its claims. Then the vocal organism, which had been principally exercised in clamoring for bodily bread, begins to demand intellectual food, asking questions and seeking answers to satisfy the mind.

Our national concern has hitherto principally regarded material interests. Our absorbing employments have been the improvement of our form of government, the organization of territories and the admission of States. When our territory shall have arrived at its ultimate enlargement, when population shall have occupied all our vacant territory, when the machinery of government shall operate everywhere without unnecessary friction, we shall be more favorably situated for intellectual labors. Then, if wealth and pride have not brought upon us fatal indolence, and if vice has not destroyed our mental and moral energies, we shall prove ourselves more than a match for "all comers" in the intellectual arena.

This being our ambition, it behooves us to give early attention to the means by which we shall accomplish our purposes. No man ever made high attainments in any intellectual pursuit who did not have his mental energies aroused in early life. If youth is spent in thoughtlessness and with unconcern for books and teachers, the maturer years will be occupied in reaching the groveling ends of mere animal existence.

Aspiring, as we do, to the high career of an intellectual nation, we should now give attention to studious pursuits, and not leave letters to be the occupation of declining years when we have become superannuated in commerce, diplomacy and war.

CHAPTER VI.

Modes of National Growth.

There is a mystery in growth. There is a problem unexplained in the blade of grass which lends its little aid in weaving for the earth a carpeting of green. There are powers therein, which so cunningly combine the elements of nature, that the closest scrutiny can not detect the secret by which they perform the miracle of growth.

The boy, whose hands are about to grasp the eggs in the birdsnest, thinks not that he is breaking a link in the golden chain of life. Did he withhold his hand, life would soon spring up within those fragile shells; and, at last, bright-plumaged birds would break forth to sing among the trees. Untaught, he would as soon suppose that the marble with which he plays would some day take wings and arouse him from his morning slumbers with a song. He learns that there is a difference, however, and inquires how and why the egg becomes a bird. The oracle—whether parent or teacher—to whom he refers, gives him an answer but little more lucid or satisfactory than the response of the Delphic oracle of old. His wise instructors have some technicalities at their tongues' ends, which pass for reasons and explanations, but in real understanding of the mystery they are but little in advance of the childish questioner.

The philosophy of the growth of nations is not so intricate and profound as that which relates to animal and vegetable life. The elements which enter into national growth are more conspicuous, their workings are more apparent. The operation has more of a mechanical character, and less of the subtle and the chemical. There is no mysterious working of a "vital force," which has been supposed to have an active agency in counteracting the ordinary course of natural causes in the animal body. An effect is usually developed near its cause, so that the least observing eye can scarcely fail to trace the connecting links. In the individual, effect often follows cause at a laggard pace, and comes up many years behind. Wild oats may be sown in youth with laborious hand, and cultivated with assiduous care, and yet many years elapse before the sower bears in his bosom the sheaves of harvest reaped in the whirlwind. "The indiscretions of youth," said Franklin, "are drafts on old age, payable thirty years after date."

National obligations to meet the consequences of indiscretion can not be deferred. They are due at date, and are presented for immediate payment. Consequently it is easy to trace the causes which harm a State, as well as to perceive the results of beneficial measures. They are the favorite topics of politicians and paragraphists in the papers. In the evil results of a mischievous measure, which is working out its speedy consequences before their eyes, they see a great supply of political capital fitted for immediate use. While the deadly nightshade of yesterday's planting and to-day's fruit-bearing, is still luxuriant, they hasten to display it to the prejudice of the person or the party that cast the seed.

If these same declaimers have done some accidental good to the State, although they may have been entirely innocent of such intent, they are not less eloquent in praise of the hardy plant of utility which has sprung up in their paths and under their crushing footsteps.

Ages were unnecessary to bring to light the disastrous effects of George the Third's insane policy toward America. Beneath his scepter, and in one of the years of his own life, his kingdom was bereft of its fairest colonies. The Terrorists of France did not have their patience exercised with waiting for children's children to rise up and claim the bloody inheritance secured by the conduct of their fathers. They were themselves ingulphed in seas, which were poured out upon France by clouds of their own brewing. Peter the Great did not die without the sight of the happy results of his royal policy. Washington and his compatriots lived to sit for many years under the Tree of Liberty which they planted.

Since, in national affairs, causes are so soon developed into unmistakable effects, there is little difference of opinion concerning *past* policy. Measures which were once advocated and opposed with a fervor so intense as to array the Nation into two great hostile parties, that contended as for life and death, are now considered as so evidently good or bad as to leave no room for difference of opinion. We sometimes wonder at the obtuseness of our good ancestors, which led them to the earnest advocacy or opposition of political doctrines, concerning whose excellence or evil all grown Americans are now unanimous.

Present and future policy is the rock on which we split. Here contingencies arise which cause these mighty disagreements, which shall make one side or the other stand in a ridiculous attitude before posterity. We are not in so favorable a position for seeing the years just before us as will be our posterity, who may turn and look backward. There are a great many opaque bodies standing in the way, which hinder and obstruct our eyesight. We think we are right, and pluck up courage to "go ahead;" yet, amid the doubts and perplexities which bewilder us, we would give a kingdom could we peer into the future.

What policies shall best promote our advancement as a nation, are vexed questions, concerning which the "doctors disagree." To settle these weighty and important issues, street-corners are made vociferous with debate, and newspapers are filled with diffuse disputations.

The safest and most beautiful mode of national growth is seen where "olive plants" spring up thickly in family homes. It does the State no harm if they grow in such close and shady contiguity as to present some obstacles to one another's uplifting trunks and spreading branches, since this may lead to their transplantation to unoccupied regions, where there is room for the penetration of their roots and the expansion of their limbs.

This is the best and safest mode of national enlargement. Even Rome, whose chief growth was from other sources, was pleased to see the increase of her population in this natural way. Citizens who were heads of large families were considered benefactors of the State. Legal disabilities were imposed upon those incorrigible specimens of perverseness who, in spite of nature and reason, persisted in singleness. Sempronia, the Roman matron, has secured to herself honorable mention in history by her celebrated exhibition of juvenile jewels, which she considered superior in value to the hoarded treasures displayed by her friend. Although the growth of Rome, as promoted by the sword, was unhealthy, yet, while such sentiments were cherished by her matrons, she could not fail to have a fountain of perpetual health and soundness in her heart.

Another normal mode of national enlargement is immigration. When a nation is as new, as free, and prosperous as ours, this stream of population will bear toward it with a current deep and wide. We would act the part of folly to place any obstruction to the free flowing of this tide.

It was numbered among the chief crimes committed against our forefathers by British tyranny that Parliament refused to pass laws for the naturalization of foreigners, and hindered their immigration hither. The colonies could not consent to forego so important a means of growth. This has been one of the chief ways by which the Republic has reached its present greatness.

For her healthy growth, it is not necessary that our country should rely on the productions indigenous to her own soil. She may find vigor in the judicious use of foreign food. The growth of Ireland and Germany should be cast into our naturalization mill, and ground as rapidly as is consistent with thorough work, and stamped with the brand "American." The aliment produced by such a process is of that nutritious kind which is greatly productive of muscular development in the body politic.

These modes of growth have proven too slow for our fast country. She has resorted to the more rapid means of annexation. Perceiving how slow a work it is, by natural and ordinary means, to "add one cubit to her stature," she has committed the extravagance of putting blocks on her head to increase her hight. She emulates the aspiring damsels of Queen Elizabeth's day, who added to their apparent stature by raising edifices of paper, paste, and vegetation on their heads. Like the fictitious and diminutive Falstaffs of the modern stage, who conceal their lack of Sir John's rotundity by the liberal use of pillows, our country has padded herself about with annexations.

If a State desires admission into the American Union, and takes proper measures to attain the honor, philanthropy would dictate to us her reception with cordial welcome. Being endowed with blessings greater than any nation before us has possessed, it would be the hight of inhumanity for us to sit down and enjoy them alone, when the friendless outcast at our door is perishing with want.

We need fear no dangerous results from annexation, if it is brought about by our sincere and prudent desire to extend the blessings of civil liberty, and not by a wicked passion for military conquest. Annexation brought about by benevolent motives will promote our natural power and greatness. It lays more broad and deep the foundations of the temple of liberty, and throws its altar of refuge more widely open to the oppressed of other shores.

Our country takes an honest pride in contemplating her own growth and advancement. Every ten years she numbers her household and makes an inventory of her goods. She sends forth her officers, who penetrate every nook and corner of the land, and by their faithful report of what they have seen and heard, they enable the nation to know her own advancement during the ten years before. From the lessons taught by such statistics, she is more competent to rule the present, and prophesy the future.

CHAPTER VII.

Of what Substance the Body Politic Consists.

The wide domain of life presents great variety of substance and structure. The lowest animals present the utmost simplicity and sameness of substance. Many marine animals, which cling to the naked rocks, and there spend an existence which can scarcely be called life, consist of matter which appears, to the unassisted sight, unorganized.

Higher life has more complicated structure, consisting of the most dissimilar tissues and organs. As the observer beholds the highest development of life on earth, and sees its multiplied forms of matter arranged in beautiful proportion, he exclaims:

"How wonderful, how complicate is man!"

The highest form of political life—our body politic—is not of such simple structure that it may be comprehended in a casual glance. It consists of a combination so curious and complex that men of thought have made it the subject of life-long study. They have returned to its contemplation day after day, through a long career, professing that every hour thus employed was laden with new knowledge.

Men have come from distant lands to see it, and have written books in foreign languages to describe its form and workings.

The particles which compose the body politic must be described in language very different from that employed by chemists concerning the ultimate atoms of matter, which, they say, are "so small that they can neither be seen nor counted, even by means of the most powerful magnifying glass."

Individual citizens are the atoms which compose the body politic.

It is a theory in chemistry that the variety in the shape and size of atoms gives rise to the various forms and phenomena of substances. The atoms of hydrogen are supposed to be very small, and hence it escapes through membranes which interpose an effectual barrier to gases of coarser grain. Crystals have their beautiful geometrical shapes, always uniform in the same substance, from a property called polarity, which regulates the sides which they present, and the way in which they adhere to one another. Gum-elastic, petroleum, and illuminating gas have the same constituent elements—hydrogen and carbon—of the same quality and equal quantity. That such different substances result from their combination is supposed to be due to the fact that the secret atoms, which elude scientific search, have certain properties and proclivities which determine the final form of the matter which they produce. They have their little tastes and affinities, which are very minute and unimportant in themselves, yet produce some marked and marvelous effects before the world.

It is fully as unfortunate for an object, so far as human comprehension and appreciation of it are concerned, when it is too small to be seen, as when it is too far removed for visibility. The two worlds—the one below the reach of microscope, and the other beyond the field of telescope—are both equally unknown. The intervening universe, especially the wide domain within reach of our unassisted bodily powers, yields the richest harvest to investigation.

Since the body politic consists of individual people, its elements are not so minute as to elude the observation of the student, and are constantly before him, demanding his attention.

They will best understand the genius of the nation who are the most diligent in the study of human nature. When a statesman thoroughly knows himself and his neighbors, he has made considerable acquaintance with the nation whose interest he is set forward to subserve. Knowing nations by the analogy of his own nature, and the deductions he draws from private character with which he comes in contact, he becomes a successful diplomatist or a wise ruler.

While it may be an unsubstantiated theory that certain phenomena of matter are dependent on the character and arrangement of the atoms, it is a principle of absolute certainty that national character depends on the physical, intellectual, and moral condition of the lively and enfranchised atoms which compose the state.

Subjects, not citizens, are the component atoms of a despotic state. People, in their noble individual characters, in their physical, mental, and moral manhood, are not constituents of such a state. Manly independence must be crushed, and personal honor swallowed up in the ravenous and insatiate state, before they can be of service in promoting the interest and advantage of the despotism. Like Saturn in mythology, despotic states devour their children as soon as they are born.

In a republic we may speak of the machinery of government, but such a term would be inappropriate in describing a despotism. Machinery is too ingeniously contrived to typify a tyrannical government. A tool is the only available instrument in the hands of a tyrant. He may avail himself of a cabinet, a senate, or an army, but they are of use to him only as means to maintain authority.

Power rests with the people, and can only be used by them, or those upon whom it is by them bestowed. Man can not create power any more than he can create matter. When the steam-engine drags the ponderous train along the iron track, or impels the oak-ribbed monster through the waves, power is developed which was created on earth many thousands of years ago. This power had its birth in the beams of the ancient sun, when they built up the luxuriant vegetation of early periods. No human being then existed to seize this power, and cause it to accomplish his purposes. But God did not allow it to run to waste. Vegetation was caused to fall into a curious current of circumstances, by which it was transformed to coal, and safely stored away to await the necessities of the human age. Now the substance is brought to light, and its hidden power applied to the accomplishment of human purposes. The giant has long slumbered, but has lost no strength by inactivity.

A bushel of coal, with its energies all brought forth and properly applied, is adequate to raising a million pounds one foot in hight. There is not here a hair-breadth more nor less of power than existed a hundred thousand years ago in the sun's rays, and in the elements of earth and atmosphere which entered into the creation of the coal.

All power at first existed alone with Almighty God. For the attainment of certain social and moral ends, he created man, and intrusted a measure of power to his hands. All men, originally and by nature, share this gift of God in a degree well-nigh the same. If, subsequently, one man rightfully possesses more power than his brethren, it is because they have bestowed it upon him, with the expectation that they shall thereby secure a greater good than by retaining it in their individual hands.

No "divine right" comes down upon kings directly from God. If they have authority from this High Source, it has reached them through the medium of the people. These are God's vicegerents, superior to all popes and princes. Under the control of Providence, this power "putteth down one, and setteth up another."

"Governments derive their just powers from the consent of the governed," sublimely spake our wise forefathers, in their immortal declaration. This "consent," withheld during so many dark and dreary centuries, has at last been given, and a government has been reared possessing "just powers," upon whose brow has been placed with glad acclaim the diadem of the world.

The running together, the combination and cohesion of thirty millions of free, thoughtful, living atoms constitutes a "royal power" in the world such as never adorned the succession of any princely house.

CHAPTER VIII.

One Head Better than Two.

A HEAD is essential to corporeal life. The possession of this member, or an approximation to it in outward shape at least, has always been regarded as essential to citizenship. One of our favorite authors has amused us with the story of "The Headless Horseman," but in actual life no one would think of appearing abroad, or laying any claims to consideration among his fellow-citizens, without sufficient attention to his toilet, to have his head in proper position.

So essential to earthly health and happiness has this member always appeared, that when a state has wished to give a last crowning mark of disapprobation to an offending subject, she has deprived him of his head.

The ancients were accustomed to number armies and populations by the head, a method of enumeration used by us only in application to our flocks and herds. More spiritually inclined, we regard man's higher nature in our computations, and in census tables we specify the number of "souls" in a city or a state.

It must not be supposed, however, that heads were held in greater honor in ancient times than now. Ancient philosophers were by no means unanimous in considering the head as the throne of reason, concerning which there is now scarcely a dissenting voice. Some supposed that the intellect had its seat in the heart, and some in the lungs; while others, with perhaps a greater number of phenomena to substantiate their inductions, supposed that human thought originated in the stomach.

Modern observers of human nature, with a unanimity truly creditable to their discernment, have chosen the head as the capital of the corporeal system. Here, according to their philosophy, the mind holds its court, and hence sends forth commands which thrill the nervous net-work of the body.

Our body politic, like every well-regulated corporeal system, is surmounted by a head, in which are concentrated our powers of thought, of will, and of action. Cerebral functions for the nation are performed in a small city on the Potomac. The situation of our political head is one-sided, and by no means favorable to symmetry and gracefulness of form. Since our political head was located, the nation has grown so rapidly in other directions, that all proportion and symmetry are lost. All modes of growth—natural increase, emigration and annexation, have operated to enlarge the West. Here the proportion of the aged and infirm is relatively small. The population is in the bloom of youth and the vigor of maturity. The wide plains and luxuriant forests invite the hardy emigrant to make himself a home. The West has developed with amazing rapidity. At the Revolution the population of the United States did not extend more than the average of one hundred miles from the sea-coast. Now the region west of the Alleghanies, in territory and population, is vastly in preponderance.

When the United States Capital was established on the Potomac, it was near the geographical center of the Union; now it is in the remote East.

It is now time that the Capital should follow the star of empire, and move westward. It behooves our country to have her chief seat in the midst of her children, whence she may readily extend her wholesome protection, where her dutiful sons may easily pay service and respect. They have gone into the wilderness and prepared the way for her; they have made the West habitable, and now invite her to make her home among them.

Many Western cities might afford to the Government a seat more honorable and more accessible than she now possesses. Their central positions, midway between the eastern and western oceans, their rapid growth, the salubrity and healthfulness of their climates, the enterprise and intelligence of their populations recommend them as proper places for the nation's Capital. Their progress thus far shows that they have other foundation for prosperity than that which results from governmental patronage. Such are their agricultural and commercial resources, that they can live and flourish without the necessity that members of Congress should expend their entire salaries in maintaining the existence and promoting the prosperity of the town.

To do service to the country, and receive honors at her hand, it should not be necessary for men to make long and tedious journeys to the obscure and distant town of Washington. Should the seat of government be removed therefrom, it would be visited by few save the curious traveler, whose eastern wanderings may have taught him to take delight in meditations among the rocks of Tyre and Nineveh, or in excursions on the Asphaltic Sea, that rolls its sluggish waves over the ancient cities of the plain.

The voice of great majorities alone should

induce good men to go and sojourn there, even for the necessary purposes of legislation. Imperative necessity alone should induce a man to expose his head to the dangers which throng the place.

The patriot goes thither as a man would rush into a burning house to bear forth his aged mother, if she lay in unconscious slumber beneath the falling rafters. Happy for him, if the garments of his honor are not burned from his body; happy if some furious firebrand does not fall upon him, and so bruise him that he must go, like Sumner, seeking restoration in other lands.

With a solemnity and sadness which were prophetical, Abraham Lincoln bade farewell to his neighbors, and left his peaceful home in Illinois, to which he was destined never to return alive. He went not in obedience to the dictates of ambition, but because the voice of Duty, of the People and of God called upon him to undergo the peril. Making part of the journey in disguise, he succeeded in performing the perilous pilgrimage. Surrounded by enemies, secret and avowed, he was defended by the Providence which rendered the Father of his Country impervious to red men's bullets. When Lincoln's sublime work had grown to its full accomplishment, the protecting Hand was, for a moment, lifted from his brow, and the evil genius of the place, ever watchful for opportunity, dealt the fatal blow, and Abraham Lincoln fell a victim to the unhappy mistake by which, many years ago, the President of the United States was doomed to make his abode in Washington.

When Hercules of old went forth to destroy the Lernean hydra, he found a unique specimen of natural history. This animal possessed remarkable tenacity of life, which greatly prolonged the conflict and rendered the victory doubtful. As soon as the hero's keen-edged blade severed a head from the body, two would spring up to occupy its place. Every blow inflicted only multiplied the foe. The assistance of a faithful slave, who kept down the multiplying heads by searing the wounds with a red-hot iron, enabled the hero to achieve at last the laborious victory.

We deprecate any analogy between the hydra and our country. Better allow our national head forever to continue as of old, if by any attempt at removal two heads should spring up in place of one.

The old adage, "Two heads are better than one," will not hold true of our body politic. For two wise men to "lay their heads together" in friendly counsel may bring about a good result; but if they are filled with antagonistic thoughts, the contact can only result in conflict. The inferior and more muscular members are drawn into conflict, in which the head loses control, and the combatants rush to most deadly extremes. The fire, kindled by the heated and impetuous brains, blazes so furiously that it can not be extinguished.

In our national person, it were better to have some doubtful deliberations and contending thoughts in an undivided head, than that two capitals should start up to espouse the championship of opposing sentiments. When one head guides and actuates the whole, no member can exert its power to harm the body, as would be possible, were they ministers to execute the furious behests of antagonistic minds. In the one case, the instinct of self-preservation guards with a fiery sword every avenue of approach to the sacred and precious life, while in the other case the overmastering impulse of love, transformed to hate, urges the powers to exterminating war.

Southern politicians endeavored to involve us in all the horrors of a divided nationality. They devised a marriage between slavery and state-rights, the fruit of which was as hideous as Milton's monster Death, the offspring of Satan and Sin. For a considerable time the monster lay coiled in comparative security in the torrid climate of the cotton states. Being covetous of the prestige which a northern habitation would bestow, it boldly put forward its slimy head, and laid it in the lap of Old Virginia. She was beguiled by the serpent, and in her infatuation fed it with food which was needed to nourish her children.

It is a matter of curious inquiry among Bible-readers how the serpent in Paradise was able to converse so humanly, and make so cunning a counterfeit of reason. Historians and statesmen in all time to come will wonder at the skillful imitation of government that was gotten up in Richmond. In Virginia, as in Paradise, there was a satanic influence behind the scenes, which furnished a portion of the impelling principle.

The serpent's head was bruised at last, and Virginia found herself with its dead carcass in her lap, but not before it had bitten many of her children to death, and blackened many of her brightest possessions with its fiery breath.

A mythological story runs that Jupiter was once afflicted with a grievous headache, and in hope of obtaining relief, he called upon Vulcan, the blacksmith of Olympus, to take an ax and cleave his skull. Vulcan begged to be excused from the murderous deed, but at last complied with the request, and brought down the ax with all the might of his brawny arm upon the serene and lofty brow of Jove. The death which would have resulted to a mortal from such a summary and heroic practice of surgery did not ensue in this memorable instance. From the fracture in the skull there leaped forth a beautiful and majestic maiden, afterward called Minerva, and worshiped as the Goddess of Wisdom.

Not until the ax of rebellion came down upon our national head, and almost cleft the cranium asunder, did Wisdom, in noble form and shining armor, appear in our national councils. That the blow which produced this parturition did not prove fatal is a proof that the nation possesses great vitality and tenacity of life. Happy is it for the nation and the world, that Wisdom, which provided for the freedom of the slave, did not prove to be a daughter of posthumous birth, born not in time to rescue her parent from the grave, but only in season to shed unavailing tears over the burial-place.

CHAPTER IX.

HARDNESS OF BONE ESSENTIAL TO UPRIGHTNESS.

In nothing do animal bodies differ more essentially than in the skeleton. From the creature of the sea, whose body consists of a viscid mass, in which scarcely a trace of osseous substance can be detected, to the upright vertebrated animal known as man, almost every conceivable variety of bony structure may be observed. Some, like the snail, carry their bones upon their backs. The oyster, whose delicate body unprotected could scarcely endure the rough ways and rude alarms of this adverse world, has his bones carefully made over into a bivalvular shell, which he wears during his sea-faring life, and never lays aside until he goes ashore to enter upon his dietetical duties.

Man pursues a different course, and modestly keeps his skeleton concealed beneath a decent exterior of cuticle and muscle. His skeleton, though very useful in a mechanical point of view, is not esthetically beautiful. It has its place behind the scenes, where invisibly it maintains the body in beautiful shape and attitude. With all its secret ghastliness, it goes forth into society, and assists in making the graceful bow of the exquisite, and the bewitching smile of the beauty.

The skeleton owes its stiffness, whereby it is able to perform useful functions, to the very common and well-known ingredient of *lime*. The limber, cartilaginous frame-work of early infancy is gradually supplied with this substantial material, until at length the skeleton has the compactness and solidity of stone.

Some ingredient analogous to lime is necessary for the uprightnesss and solidity of the frame-work of the body politic. The body must be capable of assuming a perpendicular position in case of an emergency. The lime of integrity and uprightness should enter into the composition of the body politic, otherwise it is wholly of cartilaginous structure, and becomes as "a bowing wall and tottering fence." Without this ingredient, the direful disease of moral and political "rickets" gets hold upon the frame. The bones, which should sustain the body in high and noble attitude, become as pliable as wax. The body totters beneath the weight of its own muscles, and lies prostrate, in a state of wretched imbecility. It has not strength and fortitude to escape the most imminent danger that impends, nor to make the least advance toward the greatest good that would be within easy reach of strong and sturdy limbs. It sees the furious wild beast prowling near, or the murderous highwayman approaching, without power to escape or resist. It may chance to lie near the blessed pool, and see the angel of health come down to trouble the waters, but it has no power to step in and test the healing virtue. It may even fall into the hands of wicked and ungrateful sons, who may revile it for remaining so long a useless burden on their hands. They may even consider it an act of piety to convey the helpless body to the muddy Ganges, which they worship, and cast it into the boisterous flood, while the wretched victim has not power to raise its hands to supplicate for mercy.

When a state falls a victim to such disease, her activity is ended, her career is run. She is outstripped in the path of glory by nations which once were far behind. Those that are "younger have her in derision." Beholders are amused by the ridiculous figure made by national dotage and decline, for it is well known that there is not, in the history of nations, as in the lives of individuals, a time when, by law of nature, second childhood must come on. When nations enter upon such a state, they do it simply in obedience to a law by which sins and errors eventually reap their certain retribution.

No nation presents a picture of such complete prostration and imbecility as Spain. She, who once walked abroad in uprightness and vigor, and was known and honored the world over, is now a melancholy invalid within doors. Centuries ago, when Spain was in the hight of her glory and prosperity, the Roman Catholic Church, through her obedient son, Philip the Second, prepared the muriatic acid by which the carbonate of lime has been abstracted from her bones, leaving behind only the gristly animal matter. Slowly and surely the chemical agent proceeded in its work. Soon the proud form began to feel the weakening influence. No more grand Armadas were fitted out to sail on voyages of discovery and conquest. No more brave cavaliers were abroad, conquering provinces for "His most Catholic Majesty of Spain." They were all called home and transformed into nurses and physicians, to stand around the bed of the invalid state. Being unable longer to go abroad, and make an honest livelihood (as nations count honesty) by gathering golden revenues from conquered provinces, she sold one after another of her beautiful possessions, to raise money for the ghostly fathers who administered muriatic acid, and to support physicians who knew nothing of the nature of her disease. Their remedies were all empirical, and the poor state grew gradually weaker under medicinal experiments.

At times a spasmodic energy seemed to enter her bones, and she said, "I will arise and go out as at other times before;" but she found that her "ankle-bones had not received strength," and she went but a little way beyond her own threshold. Her neighbors, who were anxious that she should have at least a "name to live," kindly conveyed her to her home again, and placed her under care of doctors. Perhaps they signified their solicitude by suggesting some root or herb, which experience had taught them was good for continuing breath in the nostrils of superannuated nations.

A contrast with this national feebleness may be seen by looking northward, where Britain has her island home. There may be seen a nationality grander and mightier to-day than ever before.

Three hundred years ago, when Philip the Second ruled Spain, and Elizabeth occupied the throne of England, the Spaniards were a mighty nation, while the English were a "feeble folk." News of an Armada fitted out by Spain filled all England with apprehension.

The weakness of England then was that of childhood. Her limbs had not become hardened with the bone and sinew of maturity. She had just abjured the Roman Catholic faith, and cast to the ground the corrosive chemical which would have eaten out the substance from her bones, and kept her in a state of worse than infantile weakness, to become the victim of a crafty hierarchy.

From that day to this she has kept a steady and discerning eye upon her bodily condition. The moment she has detected any influence at work which might ultimately destroy her, she has had courage to cast it off, however loudly the voice of false expediency might be uplifted in defense. When the incubus of slavery began to prey upon a remote part of her body, she saw at once her serious case, and adopted vigorous measures for self-preservation. By a prompt and bold operation of political surgery, she was relieved of the growing malady.

As a great maritime power, she has considered it her duty to provide that the sea should not be the medium of transmitting this disease. The principles guiding her policy at home she has carried out upon the waves. When her flag heaves in view, the horrors of the middle passage are succeeded by the delights of liberty.

Though England has a multitude of national sins which need repentance, and which the mantle of American charity can scarcely cover, yet she deserves credit for more Christianity in her politics than most of her contemporaries. She heeded the advice of such illustrious men as Wilberforce and Clarkson, and abolished slavery throughout her empire.

This was not the work of her aristocracy, but of her people—the stern and determined race that centuries before had exacted liberty for themselves from the hands of unwilling kings; the same indomitable people that in old colonial days, while struggling for existence on the bleak coast of the New World, had refused to yield the rights of Englishmen to the exactions of a king beyond the seas. The practical, hard-handed yeomanry of England set free the slaves within the limits of the British Empire. The aristocracy, with a few honorable exceptions, had no sympathy with this movement. When the Southern rebellion broke out, this portion of the English population showed that its sympathies were with slavery and aristocracy. As, by virtue of birth and precedent, they stand nearest the throne, they threw British influence into the scale, which well-nigh gave preponderance to the Southern cause.

When the masses of England gradually grew

into an understanding of the issue, they moved the resistless weight of public opinion against the defensive works of slavery, reared by the nobility, and the British nation stood once more in upright attitude, a defender of the right, an opponent of the wrong.

When in a nation's career there is wanting a bold avowal of noble principle, and open manifestation of determination to walk in the path of rectitude and virtue, the way before it is downward and easy of descent.

"Facilis descensus Averno."

It is an admirable providence which arranges the affairs of this world in such a way that, sooner or later, a nation must stumble and fall over its own crafty and unhallowed schemes. When a nation, through long habit of bending the knee, and bowing down in the presence of evil, grows weak-jointed and hunchbacked, we have reason to be thankful for the inevitable result. We see therein exercised the hand of Providence in bringing about as useful a result as when the steady shining of the summer's sun brings on the golden harvest. It is well that a nation, in the course of the commission of her deeds, is all the while making provision for their publication on her own person. If she moves continually in upright and noble attitude, every movement gives new gracefulness and strength, and promotes honorable and beautiful longevity. If with cowardly step she goes to the accomplishment of dishonorable deeds, every motion tends to mold the pliable body into more unsightly deformity.

Geological surveys reveal the fact that certain sections of our country are wanting in the lithological element whence material is obtained for stiffening backbones. The fact that the District of Columbia is deficient in limestone may account for the spinal limberness which was once prevalent among residents of that locality. Persons have gone thither possessing many noble traits of character, promising to walk in manly uprightness and integrity all their lives, and yet have yielded to the unhappy influences of the place, and made the dust the path of their tortuous and prostrate locomotion.

It has been supposed that the West, on account of its vast deposits of limestone, would produce men of larger physical proportions than other parts of the earth. It may be that, after many years, when animal chemistry has had time, by slow process, to eliminate elements from the soil, and organize them into bony tissue, the West will present specimens of humanity which shall rival the celebrated citizen of Gath. The advocates of this theory of course require time for the working out of these results, as several generations must always pass before climate, soil, and scenery can impress new peculiarities upon a people.

It may be long before the West shall impress any important physical peculiarities upon her population, but moral and intellectual influences will not be so long in manifestation. When men remove from the tainted moral atmosphere which hangs over crowded cities, and make themselves homes on the wide prairies of the West, they are brought in less frequent contact with men, and stand in closer communion with God. In great cities, men are prone to lay aside their independence and lose their moral ability to stand alone. In the performance of political functions, men are most disposed to congregate, and when one least looks for it he is liable to find himself with the multitude, obeying the behests of some noisy demagogue.

Cases are by no means rare in which men almost wholly reduced to the cartilaginous state, who were most plastic clay in the hands of the political potter, by a judicious change of climate have realized complete restoration to primitive manliness and integrity.

It is ardently hoped that the West, so favorable to solitary reflection and independent action, may have a population free from the disease we deprecate. Men can not, it is true, divest themselves of disease at will, and are sometimes compelled to wear their maladies to the remotest lands to which they wander; hence chronic cases may be found everywhere, which yield but slowly to the remedial influence of new circumstances.

Western states get out of the reach of political wires, and break away from the restraints of party leading-strings, before self-constituted nurses are prepared for such manifestations of infantile energy. The infant Hercules strangles serpents in his cradle, as a prophecy of what he shall accomplish in the maturity of his strength. Instead of spending years in the erection of cob-houses, with which his nurses and guardians desire to amuse him while they enjoy his patrimony, he kicks playthings all aside and proceeds to the erection of marble capitols. While they would hold his hand in juvenile walks, and teach him to submit implicitly to their direction, he suddenly forsakes them, and leaves them to hold the worthless remnants of their ambitious hopes.

CHAPTER X.

How Political Bone Becomes Compact.

Within the human body the change of cartilaginous substance into bone begins at certain localities called points of ossification. Here the soft and yielding substance grows compact, and rudimentary cells become parts of the solid mass which forms the frame. The work of ossification, beginning in the various parts of the body, goes on until growth in one direction meets progress in another, and at length the whole fabric is "fitly joined together."

In our body politic may be seen the bony substance in all degrees of progress—the softest gristle, the lithe and supple substance of youth, the brittle and unyielding bone of age.

In New England may be seen such stiffness and uprightness of carriage as to indicate a well-formed and thoroughly ossified skeleton. Steady habits are so thoroughly formed, that there seems to be no disposition to depart from them. New England was so carefully led in youth, by the hands of her " Pilgrim Fathers," in paths of virtue, that now neither temptations nor trials avail to lead her astray.

It would be an error to suppose that her body is kept erect by a skeleton as lifeless and unyielding as the granite of her hills. Her bone has not become a dead mineral mass, unfitted by its aged stiffness for the activities of energetic life. The vital fluid circulates freely throughout her system; the channels are not yet obstructed by the foreign substances which produce the feebleness of age. Her limbs now seem endowed with more strength to labor and more vigor to advance than ever before.

In the regions to the westward may be seen greater elasticity of limb. There is less rigidity of purpose to walk in beaten paths, and greater willingness to attempt new and untried modes of action. The American, placed a little outside the barriers of eastern restraint, claims the privilege of thinking and acting in accordance with "his own sweet will."

The western portion of the body politic differs from parts adjacent on either hand, in having neither the rigid bone of maturity, nor the cartilage of the embryonic state. While endowed with considerable vertebral stiffness, it still has power to bend; it has many well-adjusted joints which admit of easy and graceful motions.

The French element, infused by chivalrous pioneers, who sailed the northern lakes and explored the western streams, has oiled the joints, and disposed the whole apparatus to combine in making most graceful and complacent bows, on occasions which call for such demonstrations of politeness. So complacent in her politeness and so childlike and confiding in her ways has the West appeared, that designing men have presumed upon her as an easy victim of their wicked purposes.

Aaron Burr supposed he might fascinate so young a creature, and laid his plans to allure her out upon romantic enterprises, doubting not that he might at last find a pretext for riveting upon her the bonds of despotic sovereignty. The event proved the futility of such calculations upon the inexperience of the West, and showed that, although she might possess all confidence in her real friends, yet she had eyes to see and resolution to thwart the base purposes of her secret enemies.

On a subsequent occasion, calculations were erroneously made upon western pliability. Persons possessed of a peculiar kind of property, which they had found unproductive at home, desired to take their possessions to the West to see whether, as a forlorn hope, something might not be realized. There was an ugly obstacle in the way—a troublesome barrier, which shut them out of certain coveted regions more effectually than Adrian's wall prevented the approaches of the Picts and Scots to their neighbors of Southern Britain.

A design was formed of breaking down this troublesome partition. No doubt was entertained that if it could be caused to follow the example of the walls of Jericho, that Western pioneers would have no nerve to interpose obstacles to the purposes of the slave propagandists. By Congressional vote and Executive approval, the wall was spirited away, so that it has now neither a local habitation nor a name save among "the things that were." The antiquarian of time to come will search in vain along the line of its described locality to find a trace of its existence. He will not find one stone upon another to show where it stood.

Many gravely and sincerely regretted the destruction of the Missouri Compromise line, and it really seemed a national misfortune. Now there seems little in its removal to regret. Peace is a hollow thing prolonged by frowning walls. After the encroaching sin should be finally and forever swept away, and, the conflict over, brethren should dwell together in unity, the old wall would stand as an unpleasant memorial of things that it were better to forget.

Those who had seen the advancing tide of slavery roll on, with apparently resistless progress, until it reached the Line of Compromise, by which it was beaten back like surf from the rocky coast, feared that, when it should be removed, all their fair heritage would be laid waste. They did not reflect that a wall of men might be more effective than a line of legislative enactment. In some emergencies men are strangely forgetful of what they well know in cooler moments. They had read the story of Leonidas and his three hundred Spartans, and how they stood like a wall of iron against the Persian invaders; but when the lesson would have well applied and would have opened a better prospect for the future, it strangely slipped from memory. It is well that great facts and principles remain the same, despite human ignorance or inattention. Man is the material with which God erects barriers more impassable than mountain chains. He who says, "Thus far shalt thou come, and no further," has at His command the most efficient means by which the proud waves are stayed.

When the Wall of Compromise was swept away, a living barrier of men was found to subserve a better purpose. The hopes of one party and the fears of the other were alike disappointed.

The propagandists of slavery had placed great reliance upon the pliability of the young communities of the West. They had not thought them capable of so firm resistance. Not until they ran against a resistless barrier, were they aware that communities so young could have strength and firmness to resist their encroachments.

Ossification had been going steadily onward, adding firmness and vigor to more and more of the body politic. The western frontier of civilization is said to advance at the rate of fifteen miles a year. Ossification has not progressed with a regularity which admits of such accurate computation, yet it has pressed hard after the footsteps of advancing civilization. The progress of this influence bears more resemblance to the early, than the recent settlement of America. Now the army of civilization extends it long front from north to south, and marches steadily and fearlessly forward, however thin and weak may be the line. In an earlier day forts were first built far in advance of civilization, and settlements clustered about them for protection against savage foes.

The process in the body politic which is here described advances like the retarded civilization of early days. Many influences work against it. Some there are who would prefer to have our great nation lie helpless on her continental bed, a pitiable invalid, rather than see her stand, with athletic limbs, in attitude of action. They are violent in their opposition to the advancement of the elements of vigor. Being voluntary champions of imbecility and weakness, they are violent in their exertions in behalf of their feeble cause. Ossification in the body politic can only be commenced and carried on by a combination of upright and virtuous influences. Thus alone are paralyzed the hands uplifted against the advancing good.

The recent war has given great impetus to the maturing and solidifying process in the American Republic. The "shock of battle" has electrified portions of the body politic with new and nobler life. An uprightness has been given to communities which they could never have attained under old auspices.

The body politic is newly energized, and rises from the supine position in which she so long has lain. Her feet and ankle-bones have received strength. She is now capable of making greater advancement by her independent exertions, than she could have made when carried as an invalid on the shoulders of public servants, who endeavored to keep her in helpless condition, that they might bear her backward or forward, to one side or the other, as coincided with their selfish purposes.

CHAPTER XI.

PHOSPHORUS IN THE BODY—PAINS AND PLEASURES OF FIRE-EATING.

PHOSPHORUS is an element in human bones. It was discovered by the Alchemists, who called it "Son of Satan," from its fiery proclivities. This substance, in the laboratory and shop, is kept in water, because of its tendency, when exposed to air, to burst forth into flame on the slightest touch.

Of this substance, men in general have about two pounds apiece in their bodies. So carefully is it packed away in the recesses of the frame, and so well is it held in check by more sluggish substances in its neighborhood, that a fire seldom originates from this source. Life insurance companies, always distinguished for their kind scrutiny into the lurking dangers which cut short human existence, never add the fraction of a cent to their premium because the clay tenement insured is used as the store-house of so much inflammable matter.

A few years since, a portion of our body politic, though deficient in lime, was overcharged with phosphorus. Some of our fellow-citizens attained distinction as *"fire-eaters."* They are supposed to have been diligent students of human nature, and conscientious in supplying all the just demands of the bodily constitution. Being convinced that the phosphorescent ingredient in bones must need replenishing, they are supposed to have indulged in a frequent diet of coals.

He who discovers a new article of food is said to be a benefactor of his race, inasmuch as he not only adds to the means of human sustenance, but opens a new avenue of enjoyment. Among the valuable results of the discovery of America are the important additions made thereby to man's bill of fare, and the enlargement it has made to his frugal board. It is a question how our unhappy ancestors could have conducted their feasts without the dishes which America has contributed to man in our more recent and highly favored days. Did not many a guest, unsatisfied with the sameness of beef, pork, and venison, which loaded the tables of our forefathers, have a presentiment of the variety which the discovery of America would introduce into the world's bill of fare? Perhaps among the dreams which haunted our ancestors in the nights succeeding their fleshly banquets, there may have appeared some of the protean shapes which Indian corn has assumed upon modern tables.

What gratitude should inspire the hearts of all toward the man whose discernment saw in so unpromising a weed as the wild potato a staple article of food! He was endowed with genius who first conceived that the slim subterranean stems of this plant, by cultivation, would acquire such tuberous enlargement as to become available for food.

Not only in the contribution of actual articles of food has America established a claim to the gratitude of mankind, but also by the bestowal of substances like tobacco, which subserve the purposes of luxury alone. Not only does the Dutchman who has actually emigrated to the New World owe a debt of gratitude to America, but the home-keeping subject, who has never passed beyond the confines of the Fatherland, is under a heavy weight of obligation to the land which lies toward the setting sun. As he enjoys the delightsome odor which rises from the burning of his favorite leaf, and beholds the graceful garlands of smoke which wreathe the atmosphere of his room, his heart glows with gratitude toward Christopher Columbus for discovering America, and to that continent itself for the bestowal of so good a gift. The portion of his heart not preoccupied with these emotions is filled with commiseration for those unhappy people whose lives fell in the unfavored centuries when men had to breathe a vapid and inodorous atmosphere, unblessed by the fragrant incense of the pipe.

America has lately added another substance to the list of edibles. Some of her sons have sacrificed themselves to test the virtue of coals as articles of food. The experiment had the merit of self-sacrifice, as all analogy and presumption seemed to show that it would prove fatal. Up to the date of the modern achievements, history gives but a single instance of an attempt to eat burning coals—the pitiable case of a Roman lady bent on suicide. From some cause, the influence of dyspepsia in weakening the digestory organism, so that hot food could not be taken with impunity, or from over-eating, the event justified her expectation, and the unfortunate lady was gathered prematurely to her fathers.

For centuries after this event, the world supposed that the question concerning the nutritious quality of coals was decided in the negative, and experiments ceased to be made. The blistering effect of fire was so manifest on the exterior of the body, that men, ever hasty to reason from analogy, supposed that coals, if admitted into the stomach, would injure the lining membrane, and produce serious soreness of the alimentary canal.

It remained for certain Americans who won for themselves distinction as "fire-eaters" to demonstrate the fallacy of such reasoning, and show the truth of the great principle first avowed by an illustrious countryman, Mr. Samuel Patch, that "some things can be done as well as others."

They did not rashly address themselves to the perilous experiment, as did the suicidal Roman lady, but with due deliberation they proceeded to the pitch of daring to which they finally arrived.

They were careful observers of nature, and conducted their experiments according to her teachings. They observed that human habitude to certain foods is arrived at by degrees. They perceived that, by arduous effort and careful cultivation, a taste could be created for things the most repulsive.

They were aware that, by gradual beginnings, the body may be trained to do extraordinary feats. When the ancient Milo formed the bold and ambitious resolution to shoulder and carry a bull, for the amusement and instruction of his countrymen, he first applied himself to the animal when a calf, which he carried every day. Thus his strength kept pace with the growth of the animal, and at last he accomplished the wonderful feat, in the midst of admiring thousands.

There was another observation of great value to these incipient fire-eaters. They saw that man, in commencing his career of eating and digesting, does not proceed at once to solid food, but takes nourishment at first in liquid form, until the stomach acquires strength, and the necessary masticatory apparatus has been developed.

Thereupon they wisely resolved to make their first experiments upon fire in liquid form, and proceed thence to the more perilous enterprise of devouring substantial food in the form of coals. They were at no loss to find it in convenient form. They found fire in solution in a number of attractive forms, to which the highly descriptive name of "fire-water" has been applied.

Gentlemen ambitious of distinction as fire-eaters were not unfamiliar with the enlivening and exalting effects of this magical fluid. They had used it to obviate the freezing influences of winters at Washington, and found it no less potent in counteracting the fierceness of Southern heat. Had they been familiar with the language of Cicero, they would have praised their favorite beverage in the words which the Roman orator applied to literature: "It charms youth, delights old age, adorns prosperity, affords solace in adversity, drives away the dullness of home, is no hinderance abroad, spends the night with us, journeys in our company, and is the delightful companion of our retirement in the country."

As Southern gentlemen in Congress sometimes had their infallibility called in question, and frequently heard doubts expressed of the righteousness of their favorite institution, their only solace was found in the beverage which braced their nerves, and screwed their courage to the sticking point, preparatory to the performance of deeds of valor, and the infliction of bodily chastisement upon persons daring to question the superiority of the Southern people.

So important an auxiliary was whisky in such emergencies, that it was considered one of the indispensable perquisites of a Southern Congressman. In the early part of the Congressional career of John C. Breckinridge, his establishment in Washington consisted of two rooms, the principal one of which had for its only furniture a half dozen split-bottom chairs, and a keg of whisky conveniently located, with a spigot in the end, and a tin-cup hanging near. To this household god not only members of the family, but guests and strangers, were expected to pay devotions.

Persons who have conducted their explorations into the anatomy and physiology of intemperance so far as to examine the stomach of a dead inebriate, and have seen the effect which alcohol has produced on the coating of the stomach, can form some idea of the manner in which the use of whisky paved the way for fire-eating. The whole inner man became so callous that burning coals could be swallowed without a pang. The brain became so diseased by a long course of dissipation, that the mind could not act with coolness and vigor, and hence these mountebanks, bent on astounding mankind, performed the most hazardous exploits without any conception of the danger.

"What reward did they expect?" asks the practical man. This is a question which these disinterested scions of statesmanship never considered, since in all their deeds they regarded the good of the country and forgot their own interests. Statesmanship was a profession with them. Being supported by their slaves, they devoted themselves wholly to politics, and, of course, had more knowledge than other people of what would be for the country's good. Being the proprietors of this knowledge, so essential to successful statesmanship, they were, of course, incapable of employing it for any other object than the great end of government, "the greatest good to the greatest number."

Southern statesmen discovered the relation which subsisted between fire-eating and patriotism, as clearly as the idol-priests, exposed by Daniel, discerned the natural connection between worship and their own subsistence on the sumptuous banquets spread to regale their gods.

They successfully played their parts so long as Northern people could be frightened, and Southern masses held in admiration. To convince beholders that the performance was a reality and no deception, like true jugglers, they displayed the burning coals before entering upon the perilous exploit. When terror and wonder had risen to greatest intensity, the fiery morsel was put into the mouth. The physical effects were awful to behold. The cheeks were dilated to their utmost capacity; the eyes glowed as if the whole inner man were set on fire. Some of the beholders were acted upon as children hearing the nursery stories of "Raw-head and Bloody-bones." Their imaginations strove in vain to conceive how terrible it would be to fall into the hands of such monsters. The citizens of Buncombe and surrounding country were filled with admiration of their chivalrous representatives, and gratefully voted them continuance in office so long as it might please them to accept.

The fire-eaters have passed away. Their race has become extinct. Their exploits live only in history. Looking back upon their deeds, we wonder that we ever thought serious harm could happen us from their melodramatic feats. Disastrous results have come upon them and their followers. The flames kindled by their fiery exhalations have ravaged the entire South, and left her fair fields a waste of ruin.

The mind will sometimes amuse itself by attempting to conceive the state of things, had fire-eaters succeeded in demonstrating the excellence of coals as an article of food. They would have been held in honor as benefactors of the race. The question, "What shall we eat?" asked and unanswered so many times in every age, which has driven countless multitudes, in every generation, to lives of unmitigated toil, would have found satisfactory reply. Butchers would have been supplanted by colliers, and firemen would occupy the place of cooks. The fire-alarm would fall on the ear with as grateful sound as dinner-bells. Hungry people would gather round a conflagration, and feast upon firebrands with unalloyed delight. Shovel and tongs would occupy the place in daily use now held by knife and fork. The coal-fields of Pennsylvania would be "The garden-spot of America." Newcastle would furnish a vast cellar stored with food to satisfy the hungry population of Great Britain.

In view of the rapid increase of the human race, political economists have expressed concern for the dense population of future times, fearing lest the fruitful earth may not yield food for the countless millions that shall swarm the continents. Had the feasibility of fire-eating been fully shown, all such concern would forever have been set at rest. Surely the morrow might be left to "take thought for itself," since there are five thousand billions of tons of coal in the earth, besides eight hundred thousand millions of tons of carbon floating in the atmosphere, in an invisible state, waiting to go down through the avenues of vegetation to augment the exhaustless treasure.

Had all these stores of carbon in the earth and air been found available for food, specters of Famine and Starvation would be forever banished from the abodes of men. Unfortunately, however, fire-eating is no longer considered a practicable thing, and is numbered among the exploded bubbles of former years.

CHAPTER XII.

National Nerves—Their Former and their Latter Uses.

The human body without means of communication between the different parts would be unwieldy and useless matter. There could be no unity of action. The most deadly harm might prey upon a limb, and no information could reach the seat of intelligence, and no sympathy or assistance come from other members.

Our bodies are not thus left to become a prey to destruction. A delicate system of nerves is laid in the body, threading the frame everywhere with its curious channels of communication. Upward and downward, backward and forward, right and left, lie these secret avenues of sensation and volition, ready to transmit to and from the mind, with telegraphic swiftness, all matters of moment to the bodily health and safety.

If, by any misfortune, the nerves of motion and sensation in a limb are paralyzed, it hangs languid and lifeless, a hinderance rather than a help. The mind which before animated it, and the fellow members which were wont to run swiftly to its help, grow indifferent to its welfare. Having resigned it sorrowfully to premature death, they take no more trouble nor concern for its safety.

When the nervous system is all in working order, it forms a most complete and efficient source of safety. When, by the blunder of an awkward arm, a finger is thrust into danger, news of the harm is quickly conveyed to the brain. "I burn," is telegraphed by the injured member to head-quarters. The fire-alarm sounds in an instant throughout the body. Motory nerves are used to acknowledge the receipt of the intelligence, and at the same time to give directions concerning the means of safety. The muscles are acted upon, and by their strong and efficient aid the injured part is lifted from the midst of harm, and placed beyond the reach of danger. If desirable, the whole body is put in motion, and placed as far as possible from harm.

A nervous system is essential to the health and safety of the body politic, for without it our country would be little better than contiguous masses of plains and mountains.

Our postal system forms an important part of the nervous net-work of the body politic. Its motory and sensitive threads are distributed throughout the land. From the Atlantic to the Pacific, from the Northern lakes to the Southern Gulf, there is no spot to which its messages may not penetrate. There is no citizen so obscure or so distant that he may not be reached by its far-extending influences.

This apparatus was originally constructed that facilities might be afforded the inhabitants of the country for communicating with one another. It occurred to those who constructed our Government, that man is a social being, and is prone to remember his absent friends. It moreover seemed extremely desirable that the separation of a few miles should not make enemies of those who would otherwise be friends. Ability to drop an epistle to a distant friend would do much to render the pioneer on the Western frontier contented in his wilderness abode. It would do much to bind the lover and the tradesman by ties of affection to their country, to know that easy and cheap facilities were afforded by its ample provision for sending messages of affection and business to sweethearts and to customers.

The National Government early took into her own hand the work for which she alone was adequate. She then had a single eye toward the happiness of the people. Unsophisticated as she was, she did not dream that the selection of servants to accomplish her beneficent purposes would open to them the floodgates of fortune. Unreasonable as it may now appear, her design was not to confer honor or emolument upon the office-holder, but to employ the best means for accomplishing her kind intentions toward the people.

Soon the office of postmaster became the object of loud clamor and laborious effort:

> "For never office yet so mean could prove,
> But there was eke a mind which did that office love."

Multitudes were found willing to forego a good conscience and an honest employment to enjoy the few scanty loaves and diminutive fishes doled to hungry beggars at the door of the Post-office Department. The paltry pence picked up in this way were at par value with persons whose tastes and habits unfitted them for the laborious duties of an independent employment, and the honor was an emolument highly prized by persons whose private resources in this particular were limited.

On the eve of a Presidential election there are thousands who hope that they are the favored ones for whom fortune will next turn up a prize. They grow extremely solicitous for the welfare of their country. There is nowhere in all the world so redoubtable a knight as the Quixotic hero to whom these Sancho Panzas have attached their fortunes, in hopes that the long-looked-for "island" may be obtained at last. English lexicography is taxed to the utmost to furnish words expressive of the superlative purity of the patriotism, and the transparent integrity of the candidate whose claims they advocate. If their candidate is elected, they estimate every one of these ponderous epithets as "worth its weight in gold."

The Presidential contest is scarcely over, and the smoke of battle has not cleared away, before the ardent patriots, whose exertions have won the day, give over their efforts to save the Union, and hasten to secure the reward of their disinterested services. The head-quarters of the successful faction now suffer siege. The incoming administration may well pray to be "saved from its friends." The camp, where erewhile was the utmost harmony of action, is now uproarious with contention concerning the division of the spoils. Every man's hand is against his neighbor. Only when the office-seeker's own ambition is fully gratified, is he ready to assist his comrades in arms.

Many are disappointed, while some go away

with ambition, for the present, satisfied. If they preserve their party allegiance, and set a strict watch over all their words, they may preside over post-offices for at least four years succeeding. As the administration conferring the favor has the battery of patronage, which it may bring to bear in the next contest, there is a pleasing probability that they may get a renewed lease of life. Their tenacity of life is strong. Even in the "hour and article of death," they do not yield up the ghost without a fierce struggle with the grim monster. They are willing to purchase a respite or release on any terms.

A certain queen, in the closing scene of her career, in view of unrepented sins, expressed her willingness to give her kingdom for a single hour to live. If office-holders wished a further term of life, that they might have space for repentance, and time in which to manifest its sincerity by honest practices, there would be great propriety in their tenacity of life.

The original design of the post-office was to afford citizens of the country facilities for communication. This end has assumed a secondary place. The primary object now seems to be to render every portion of the body aware of Presidential will, and submissive to executive mandates. The President has certain sentiments, the dissemination of which he considers of vital importance to his own personal good, and the advantage of the party for whose benefit he rules. He finds the post-office an efficient means of disseminating these sentiments to the remotest part of the republic. Not that the President avails himself of the post-office, as a plain citizen would do, by writing his convictions in a letter to a correspondent in Maine or California, and sending it by mail to its remote destination. In no such commonplace manner as this does the President employ the post-office. The line of duty is peremptorily laid down to postmasters, in which they must walk with undeviating directness. The details of partisan tactics are carefully taught them, and they must obey all orders with military exactness.

Woe to the unfortunate official who dares to dilute pure Presidential instructions with unreasonable scruples of his own! He has wandered beyond the tender mercies of executive clemency. The sword breaks the slender hair upon which it has hung; the ill-starred official head drops into the basket.

CHAPTER XIII.

OUR MAIN ARTERY AND ITS IMPORTANT FUNCTIONS.

An observer, looking down from some aerial hight upon North America, would have his attention attracted by what would seem to be a woof of silvery threads permeating the continent beneath. At first the system and symmetry would not appear, and the threads would seem distributed and combined at random. A more careful survey, however, would make it apparent that the smaller lines are interwoven with one of larger dimensions threading the great central valley.

This is not a piece of silver lace-work thrown over the continent for purposes of ornament alone. It forms our great fluviatile circulation. The eye of the observer, tracing the great central stream northward, at length reaches a locality bearing resemblance to Eden, as described in Scripture. As many streams as those which flowed from Paradise there gather their crystal waters, and hasten on their several ways—one through a chain of lakes to the Atlantic; another through Western plains to the Pacific; a third to

Hudson's Bay; and the last and greatest, flowing southward, conveys its waters to the Gulf of Mexico.

The region where these rivers take their rise is the "heart of the continent," whence flow the great arteries which animate and beautify the Western world. The Mississippi, distributing verdure and beauty along its banks, and contributing to the prosperity of the populous states through which it flows, is the main artery of the great fluviatile circulation.

There is analogy between the arterial system of the body and the rivers which build up and irrigate a fertile country. Rivers acted an important part in preparing the globe for its present uses. They gathered and assorted materials, and distributed them to form the picturesque and fertile surface of the earth.

Some countries were made by the rivers which run through them. Egypt has been called the "gift of the Nile." But for the early and assiduous efforts of this mighty river, the site of Egypt would now be occupied by sea, and but for its later labors of irrigation, the country would be but a sandy desert.

As the blood, animated by contact with the outer world in the lungs, and urged to hot haste by a brief visit to the heart, goes forth to the remotest parts of the body, bearing new particles of vigorous life, which are deposited where there may be great need, or extraordinary labor in process of performance, so rivers not only distribute new soil upon spots where fertility had been destroyed by many harvests, but, commercially, they remove the surplus productions of the fertile shores, and bring back in return precious cargoes from other climes.

Rivers are indispensable to great and prosperous populations. No favorable situation on the sea-shore can compensate for the want of direct and continuous communication with the interior.

The Mississippi was regarded as so important a possession, that Spain, France, and England all set up their several claims to the great river and the valley through which it flows. The Spaniards called it "Rio Grande," and the French "St. Louis," but neither of these names was so appropriate as the Indian title by which it is now known. The powers of Europe that laid claim to the elephantine prize were at a loss to know where or how it should be kept. Had it been reckoned among their movable effects, the narrow homesteads of England, France, and Spain would not have sufficed for its safe-keeping, unless it could have been coiled after the manner of a serpent. In such a case these countries would have the river as their sole possession, to the exclusion of their old and boasted landed property. Even Spain, if she survived the deluge, looking over her watery domain, might claim England's self-arrogated title, "Mistress of the Sea."

Happily for the permanence of those old European countries, and the prosperity of the American Continent, rivers, although constantly in motion, are not reckoned among movable effects. Consequently, when European nations moved back to their old dominions, or collected their household goods into more limited settlements upon this continent, they bade a final farewell to the Father of Waters, and he became once more, as he had been in the beginning, an exclusively American river. The new proprietor is possessed of ample territory for the sports and labors of the great river and all its attendant streams.

This great American artery, originating in the heart of the continent, as it flows through Northern hills and plains comes in contact with a thoroughly purified and oxygenized atmosphere. It conveys along its widening and deepening channel abundant means whereby the country develops strength. On its waters float the productions of the Northern plains. These find a lodgment in Southern markets, or go to supply distant quarters of the globe.

Blood is a mysterious thing. After long chemical and physiological research, men are unable to explain all the influences by which health and disease lurk within the crimson tide. Powers work silently and invisibly within its hidden streams, nor do they divulge the secret of their presence until disease breaks forth with boldness and asserts its sway, or a better spirit, Hygeia, the impersonation of health, with powers fully developed, leaps up to occupy the vacant throne, whence her athletic arm hurls headlong her disgusting rival.

The celebrated plague of Egypt has not been inflicted upon American rivers. Our worse than Egyptian obstinacy, in refusing to let our bondsmen go, did not quite provoke the Almighty to turn the waters of our rivers into veritable blood. The sword had opened fountains of blood in patriotic hearts, which had begun to dye the waters of our rivers, when the Emancipation Proclamation, setting the bondsmen free, gave a solution of our national troubles, before we had reached the full measure of the ancient curse.

As the heart transmits blood along the arteries to some languid and unhealthy limb, until by degrees it is restored to soundness, so an element of health is mingled with the waters of the Mississippi, and goes onward in its ceaseless flow.

The intellectual vigor, the enterprise, the freedom of the North are flowing southward with the waves of the Mississippi. They are destined to overflow the valley, from the Northern lakes to the Southern Gulf. No Southern levees shall prevent, no state boundaries shall prove an effectual barrier. The very force of gravity, by which the waters seek the level of the sea, bears this influence toward its destination.

The infatuated people attempting to dam the Nile with bulrushes, in the eloquent hypothesis of a celebrated orator, find a parallel in persons who put forth their frantic efforts to obstruct the progressive principles borne onward with the tide of the southward-flowing river.

Xerxes, one of the largest and most foolish slaveholders of antiquity, had, like most of his craft, great faith in shackles. Since his experience had proven that they were sovereign remedies for all human obduracies and evils, his profound analogical reasonings led him to the conclusion that they would likewise be effectual with inanimate nature.

When the Hellespont dared to despise his royal authority, and break with its billowy arm his bridge of boats, Xerxes commanded his blacksmith to prepare shackles with which to bind the turbulent and uproarious subject. The blacksmith must have been at a loss into what form to shape his iron. He had often made manacles for limbs of ordinary human dimensions; but when an "arm of the sea" so sturdy as the Hellespont was to be fitted with chains, all his previous measurements and models were at fault. The king's command was urgent, however, and shackles were forged whose exact dimensions have not come down to present times.

The redoubtable king caused the chains to be brought forth with a pomp and publicity which added greatly to the weight of the punishment. It was proper that a public example should be made, lest other and even smaller straits should grow refractory, and dare to set at naught the royal authority. With some weighty words of royal reproof, the shackles were cast into the rebellious strait. The metallic morsel was received into the sea's remorseless mouth, but the waves ceased not to toss as wildly and roar as loudly as before.

King Xerxes gave evidence, on this occasion, that even a long course of tyrannical rule does not dry up all fountains of feeling in the human breast. As he sat on his marble throne, he was deeply affected to see his royal authority so boldly set at naught by an insignificant sea, in the presence of more than a million men, and he shed tears of heart-felt grief. A courtier, with many salaams and expressions of deferential awe, inquired the cause of the royal tears. The king would have felt humiliated to unveil the feelings of an ordinary mortal to a courtier, hence he cloaked them by saying that he wept to think that in one hundred years all that vast multitude would be numbered among the dead. This, certainly, was a thought sufficiently melancholy for tears, especially since the poor king reflected that his own royal head must lie low among the rest. The conclusion can not easily be resisted, however, in view of the nearness in time and place of the irrepressible rebellion of the Hellespont, that the king wept rather from mortification that in the royal presence a body of water should exhibit such decided and boisterous preference for liberty.

The great lesson taught by the case of Xerxes is the folly of even a despot's trying to war against nature, and resist the solemn progress of human destiny. Shackles, whether attached to bodies of water, arms of the sea, or limbs of men, can have but a temporary power, and possess a resistless and inherent tendency to break in pieces. Any attempt to curtail the ancient liberties of nature, or of man, must prove abortive, and speedy failure must crown all ambitious efforts in this direction.

When a great and free-born river, like the Mississippi, persists in flowing toward a particular point of the compass, even though it comes laden with principles the most hostile to peculiar local institutions, the wisest course for all concerned is to allow it a steady and unresisted flow. All attempts to resist it are the hight of folly. An army of obscure fellow-craftsmen and petty emulators of Xerxes could not stay the river in its advances. It must flow onward, bearing in its bosom a great transforming and rejuvenating power.

It was a custom in the South, in days anterior to the civil war, to consider newspapers containing sentiments opposed to slavery as incendiary documents and commit them to the flames. Consistency would have voted, for similar reasons, the Mississippi an "incendiary" stream.

Chemists have been searching, with all the zeal of the old alchemists, to discover the secret influence by which the miracle of setting fire to water may be wrought. Philosophers have predicted that science will at no distant day render the economy of power so great, that one-half of a gallon of water may be used to convert the other half into steam. Such a result may crown the labors of a wiser and more skillful age than ours; meanwhile nervous people of low latitudes may be relieved of fear that a Northern river will kindle a conflagration among their cotton-fields.

A long course of uniformly consistent action leaves no doubt as to the political proclivities of the Mississippi. However politicians may "box the compass" in their attempts to go with the tide of popular favor, the great river changes not its course, but flows on, true as ever to the great principles of Liberty and Humanity.

The Mississippi pours into the sea one hundred and one cubic miles of water every year. Mingled with this vast flowing sea are nearly thirty billions of feet of solid matter from the north, which is partly distributed along its shores, but principally deposited to augment the great delta which continually encroaches upon the sea at its mouth. With unceasing labor it is extending the area of the continent, having already, by its own constant and stupendous exertions, built up an extent of country thirteen thousand square miles in area, and one thousand feet in depth.

This river has ever been the most efficient and active promoter of free-soil policy. While politicians talked in loud and lengthened strains concerning their various schemes of public policy, the grand and silent river was occupied in action. It labored so mightily, in combination with the brave and earnest men who dwelt on its Northern banks, that new policies, new laws, and new religions have been established along its lower shores. The great laws of moral and physical gravitation, acting together, have carried freedom to the utmost reach of the Mississippi's waves.

In view of the physical structure of our country, a division of the Union by a line running east and west, which would sever the great artery of our life and commerce, would be a fatal operation. Political life could not survive the terrible dissection. Both sections would be smitten with the stroke of death. The half wherein the heart is situated might make a few spasmodic struggles to retain the breath of life, but unless reunion could be speedily secured, it would soon subside into the embrace of death.

It is plainly written as a law of nature, that one nation must possess the Mississippi from its source to place of disemboguement. Jefferson perceived the force of this physical and political principle, and in becoming the purchaser of Louisiana he conferred upon the West a favor almost as signal as when he penned the Declaration of Independence.

When the wise king in olden time decreed that the child, for which two women desired to perform maternal offices, should be divided between the contending parties, the true mother would not consent to the dissection, and finally had the happiness to bear away her undivided offspring.

We have recently seen a similar event, on a grander scale, in the controversy between the North and South. The fictitious mother, who had no part in the origin of the stream, who had contributed little of her money for the purchase of the territory along its banks, was clamorous for division; but the North, with true maternal instincts, so bravely and effectually lifted voice and hand against the measure, that she finally carried off the undivided prize.

CHAPTER XIV.

Our Landed Estate, and How We Have a Rich Uncle.

A people claiming recognition as a state, without territorial domain, would be as unreasonable as a spirit that should attempt to take part in the labors and struggles of this world after "shuffling off this mortal coil."

Archimedes required a place whereon to stand as a necessary precedent to the performance of his celebrated feat of moving the world, a work which he never accomplished, from the fact that people thought the globe had motion enough in the old and natural way, and never went to the trouble and expense of furnishing the philosopher with the stipulated standing room.

Many an ambitious man has considered himself capable of founding an empire, if he could have room and verge for carrying out his plans. Many a brave people has had its grand schemes of empire thwarted by the rude unwillingness of some stronger race to allow it the use of a free and unincumbered soil.

Since "a local habitation" is essential to the

enjoyment of a national "name," the question how territory may be acquired has always been among the first subjects demanding practical consideration by an incipient nation.

"Let us get territory—honestly if we can, dishonestly if we must; any way, let us have territory"—has been the practical maxim of all nations. When Dido, first Queen of Carthage, set forth to found a little kingdom, she struck a bargain with a sturdy African landholder for so much ground as she could cover with a bull's hide. The vender, unused to the sharp practice of land speculators, supposing that the woman could have no other design in the purchase of so small a piece of land than to make a burial place, sold the ground for a paltry sum. What was his astonishment to see the woman cut the bull's hide into narrow strips and stretch it over land enough for a little kingdom! Having been outwitted by a woman, he had the gallantry to submit and acknowledge the legality of the sale.

A great many ambitious men have carved empires for themselves out of other people's land. Their titles to their blood-bought possessions have been respected so long as they have been able to hold the sword firmly in their hands.

Their "most Catholic and Christian majesties" of modern Europe have held the doctrine that discovery gave them the right of possession. In sending forth their ships of discovery toward the west, adventurers were supplied with crosses and colors, which they piously and patriotically erected on whatsoever lands they discovered, thus taking formal possession for their sovereigns. The native Indians, being pagans, were not supposed to have any rights which Christians were bound to respect.

Spain, England, France, Portugal, and Holland claimed the Western Hemisphere as their rightful possession, and since

"Their right there was none to dispute,"

except a few naked and unarmed savages, they had no great trouble to maintain their claims.

Happily for the interests of North America, England asserted and finally made good her claim to the country lying along the Atlantic coast from Maine to the Carolinas. The land was considered, immediately on its discovery, as the property of the Crown. Fortunately for the interests of mankind, kings are generally poor, and are often under the necessity of resorting to various expedients for the purpose of raising money.

The debts and embarrassments of the kings of England induced them very soon to dispose of their "Western lands" in various ways. Sometimes they sold out extensive tracts to individuals, as Pennsylvania to William Penn, and Maryland to Lord Baltimore. Again they sold to corporations, as the New England Colonies and the Carolinas. Sometimes, as in the case of Virginia, the King retained ownership, and considered the colonists as his tenants.

The King, however, claimed more or less control over the territory of all the colonies, until our sturdy forefathers made good their right to be absolute and independent proprietors.

People are sometimes very liberal in gifts and sales, if they have paid but little for what they sell, or have but an uncertain title. So the Kings of England, in their charters to proprietors and colonies, generally conveyed all the land stretching westward to the Pacific Ocean. The consequence was that the vast forests and prairies of the West were "shingled over" with colonial claims. The claims of Virginia, New York, Pennsylvania, and Connecticut were so tangled and interlaced that no human art could ever have "untwisted the twist," had not Congress cut the Gordian knot by requesting the states to cede all their unoccupied lands to the General Government for the benefit of the whole. The states gracefully complied.

New York was the first to acquiesce; Virginia followed the example, and soon all the states had transferred to the General Government their claims to unoccupied lands.

The "Records of the World" have very few deeds registered in them which set forth transfers of such magnificent estates. In this exhibition of magnanimity on the part of his children, Uncle Sam laid the foundation of his vast wealth, which has so frequently dazzled the eyes of his hopeful nephews, and induced them joyfully to sing:

"Uncle Sam is rich enough to give us all a farm."

They have generally realized the fate of other nephews and nieces who have built great expectations upon the wealth of rich uncles. Very few have got farms from Government without having first made good their titles by their honest labor.

Many people have a passion for buying land, and, no matter how large may be their possessions, they are always willing to buy an "adjoining farm." Our good Uncle Samuel has manifested the same proclivity, and has bought nearly all the land around him. He paid $5,000,000 to Spain for Florida, and took upon himself the task of driving the wretched Seminoles out of its dismal swamps, which made the purchase cost him several millions more.

He paid $15,000,000 for Louisiana. As this purchase gave him the mouth of the Mississippi, and furnished free outlet and inlet for the vast river commerce of the West, it was a good bargain.

Texas, having cost $10,000,000 and a bloody war, proved a dear purchase, as the land was hardly paid for before the demented dame of the "Lone Star" packed up the entire property, personal and real, and attempted to walk off with it, much to the disgust of Uncle Samuel, who was compelled to expend about three thousand millions of dollars to get her and her plunder back again.

California and New Mexico were bought by a large outlay. Happily for our fortunes, the old Spanish and Mexican proprietors had stumbled over the precious metals of the Western valleys, without dreaming that they walked in their sleep in Aladdin's cave Soon after the acquisition of California, immense gold deposits were discovered, and our good uncle correctly thinks he made a "lucky strike."

Our excellent uncle has never been mean or miserly in the management and distribution of his vast estates. It was first suggested by some of his selfish advisers, that he ought not to pother his brain with the petty annoyance of peddling out his land at retail, that he should sell in tracts of not less than one township in extent. He was deluded into a short and unwilling compliance with this suggestion; but the kindliness of his generous heart soon assured him that this policy was unwise. It was ungenerous and unkind to the poorer people, whom his instincts taught him needed most his parental care. He immediately resolved to sell in quarter sections. Afterward, with the same benevolent intent, he further subdivided into eighth, and finally into sixteenth sections, so that men whose means were limited might buy a farm of forty acres.

Our great governmental landholder has not kept his lands for speculation, nor has he held them at such prices as to place them beyond the poorest of the population. His regular price has been one dollar and a quarter per acre, and when lands have been long upon his hands unsold, he has adopted a graduated scale of prices, running as low as twelve and a half cents.

He has adopted the wise and liberal policy of giving farms to those who have served as soldiers in his wars. Finally, in 1862, he solemnly ordained that any person who should become an actual settler on his unoccupied domain should have a free gift of one hundred and sixty acres.

For states, as well as for individuals, the General Government has devised liberal things. When it appeared that large tracts of public land in many of the states were marshy and productive of pestilence, such lands were given to the states in which they lay, that prompt measures might be taken for their drainage and cultivation.

It is a part of the compact under which each new state has been admitted, that it shall not tax public lands within its limits. As a consideration for this exemption from taxation, a section in every township has been given for school purposes, and five per cent. of all sales of public lands has been paid into the state treasuries.

In view of the terms under which the public lands were originally accepted of the states, it is improper for Congress to appropriate public lands in such a way as shall not benefit all the states alike. Hence the folly of the persistent begging which is frequently indulged in at the door of Congress, for slices of the public land for the promotion of schemes of local interest.

It may be prudent and proper for the General

Government, like any other landholder, to give part of a possession to augment the value of the rest; hence the appropriation of lands for the construction of important railroads is the dictate of sound policy. He who cajoles the Government into large appropriations for the promotion of mere local schemes is practically a robber of the public treasury.

After all the sales which have been made during three-quarters of a century, yielding a revenue of two or three millions of dollars per annum, and all the princely gifts which have been made for purposes wise and otherwise, there yet remains in the possession of our great governmental proprietary a domain of nearly fifteen hundred millions of acres.

No territory could be better adapted to the wants of a great people than that which lies between the Atlantic and Pacific Oceans, and stretches its vast extent through the latitudes which lie between the Northern lakes and the Mexican Gulf. The Atlantic slope, embracing the territory between the Alleghanies and the Eastern sea, afforded scope and verge enough to exercise all the powers of the nation's early life. When maturer powers and activities demanded a wider field, the vast valley of the Mississippi opened its realms of exhaustless fertility. To perfect and complete our bodily form, and give us dimensions worthy of our character and destiny as a people, the Pacific slope became a beautiful and symmetrical part of our national domain.

Political geography treats of the earth in reference to its artificial divisions and distinct nationalities. Physical geography regards the great natural characteristics of the globe, and knows nothing of the colored pictures on maps and globes, which men call states and kingdoms. The contour of the continents, both lateral and vertical, the characteristics of climate and soil, the direction of prevailing winds and currents of the sea, are subjects which demand the attention of the physical geographer.

After territorial limits are fixed, and the political map is properly adjusted, a nation has more concern in its physical than in its political geography. As an element with which to estimate the character of a nation, the climate, the altitude, the sea-coasts, the plains, and mountain ranges have more to do than the territorial extent. The island of Britain, washed by the northern seas, and indented with harbors, is a more important portion of the globe, and nurtures a mightier race, than the vast continent of Africa, with its smooth line of coast, unfavorable to commerce, and its vast and unexplored expanse of arid waste.

He who would thoroughly understand the character of an individual man must know something of his physical organism—whether it is fragile or robust, diseased or sound. He must know whether he has nervous, sanguine, or lymphatic temperament. He who would know a national character should inform himself as thoroughly as possible concerning the peculiarities of the land in which the nation lives.

That a man may successfully treat with a foreign nation, or honorably reside as a diplomatist at a foreign court, he should have some acquaintance with the language of the people with whom he has to deal. Knowledge of equal value and higher necessity is that which relates to the physical characteristics of the people and their land. Furnished with such knowledge, he can balance the peculiarities of the nation with whom he treats, by those of the people for whom he acts.

Scenery and climate have much to do in accounting for English persistency, French impetuosity, Swiss liberty, Italian softness, and American enterprise.

A beautiful body and affluent fortune sometimes seem at variance with the highest moral and intellectual traits, as serene skies and fields of exhaustless fertility do often depress rather than elevate a people.

In the American country the beautiful and the excellent greatly predominate, yet there is a sufficient admixture of the rough and incorrigible to deplete our pride. Nature is not so lavish with her spontaneous productions that industry becomes a foreign and unnecessary virtue. Men here must lay aside the gaudy garments of aristocratic pride, and labor for daily bread.

In giving this country to the American people, the Divine Being pursued a policy similar to that which characterized the distribution of wine in the marriage feast. The rougher localities were first opened to settlement and civilization, while the fruitful and salubrious plains of the West were withheld until the wilderness of the East was caused to bloom. Had these flowery and fertile prairies been opened for husbandry a hundred years ago, the patient plowman had not been content to cultivate the stony acres of the East, and those now smiling abodes of wealth and beauty had been abandoned to hopeless sterility.

Our long and deeply indented lines of seacoast, our vast rivers, our great lakes, our fertile plains, our lofty mountains, all combine to form a physical structure admirably fitted to be the bodily abode of the American Republic.

CHAPTER XV.

Folly of Affection for a Part and Hatred of the Whole.

Montesquieu affirms that a republican government is adapted only to a small territory, and that a large extent of country can only be well governed as a monarchy. He says that sectional jealousy must inevitably overthrow a republic possessed of large domain.

The history of the United States is at variance with the theory of the French philosopher, and has solved the problem by which the largest territory may be united as one body politic. A community of states, united under one general government, gives to every section the power of governing itself by laws adapted to its local circumstances, while the grand combination of commonwealths presents such a powerful presence before other nations, that security from foreign aggressions is obtained, and perpetuity of national existence realized.

Sectional prejudice is a most unreasonable folly

in the American people. A particular feature of the human body may be regarded with more admiration than others, and may possess points of beauty and utility denied to fellow-members, yet no ill-will is cherished toward the less favored parts. Pain may penetrate a portion of the body, revealing the presence of disorder, and there may arise in the mind serious thoughts of desperate remedies for the removal of disease, without the least ill-feeling toward the disabled part.

The ancient fable of the "Belly and the Members" teaches an excellent moral, and yet, in the details of the narrative, it is romance rather than reality. The members of the body, in real life, never engage in vain disputations, nor break out into open hostility. They have not such sense of self-sufficiency as would prompt them to carry on a controversy. No man in waking moments has ever heard his hand, in angry expostulation with his foot, say, "I have no need of thee!" Such scenes transpire only in parable.

The nation endowed with ordinary instincts of self-preservation, and possessed of suitable pride of character, will not submit to the ordeal of amputation. He who shall boast his ability to perform this feat of political surgery, and attempt to give practical exhibition of his skill, should incur the odium and the penalties of treason.

The limbs "fitly joined together" will, in all time to come, refuse to be separated, and prefer to walk along the dusty path of future life in company. Their mutual assistance and sympathy will beguile the long journey of its tediousness, and render effectual every effort to remove an obstacle and surmount a barrier. When the nation "lays down her arms" she will be on her "last legs;" her race will be run and her career accomplished.

In such a sad event, her burial-place should be at the cross-roads, where suicides were interred in olden times. Shapeless heaps of stones were piled over their graves, to attract the attention of travelers, and excite abhorrence of the inhuman crime which brought them to such disgraceful end.

Similar should be the last and eternal resting-place of our dead nationality, since no human hand has power to take her life except with her own coöperation and consent. She alone, dwelling in the impregnable fortress where her life is guarded, has power with the murderous steel to reach the secret springs of her vitality. She alone has power to direct the spark of conflagration so that it may fall upon the explosive material hidden away in the most secret recess of her citadel.

The cry of "Sectionalism," often raised to terrify men and drive them from adherence to cherished principles, is a word most sadly abused and ignorantly misunderstood. Nothing but the most willful perversity would brand a man with "sectionalism," because he advocates doctrines which are popular in one locality and odious in another. Great principles, whether of physical or political science, have existence independently of time and place. They remain steadfast, though every empire of the earth were swept away, and every mountain carried into the midst of the sea.

He who becomes the disciple of such principle follows no *ignis fatuus*, which flies with the shadows at the dawn of day. It shall outlive the earth where it has its temporary field of application and development, and shall forever honor him who was its advocate during the mundane years of its unpopularity.

There can be no "sectionalism" in advocating principles as wide in their application as the universe. There is "sectionalism" in assuming the championship of doctrines which have their chief popularity in Pandemonium, and are limited in their sway to places where the powers of darkness rule. There is "sectionalism" when a citizen puts on pride because of Massachusetts or Virginia birth; but none in advocating the great principles of Truth, though their application should disturb the moral and mental repose of half an empire. There was "sectionalism" when Hayne and Webster made great orations concerning the amount of glory which South Carolina and Massachusetts should respectively possess in consideration of their services in the Revolution. There was no "sectionalism" in the bold defense of the Right of Petition, uttered by John Quincy Adams on the floor of Congress; nor yet in the opposition which certain champions of Truth presented against the Fugitive-slave Law, when they declared it contrary to the principles of Christianity and the rights of man. In this defense, and in this opposition, there was true and expansive patriotism, loving the whole country, and sorrowing for sins in which all are implicated, and yet a part reap the most direct effects and bitter fruits.

Now, that the civil war is over and the arrogant dogma of State-rights has gone down amid the storm of battle, we may expect that the local jealousies which have so long divided the people will soon disappear. The foolish passion called "State pride" is unworthy of strong-minded, patriotic Americans. It should be left to eke out the scanty intellectual treasures of him who

"Never had a dozen thoughts in all his life,"

and thinks

"The visual line that girds him round, the world's extreme."

CHAPTER XVI.

How Deadly Disorder is Contracted and Cure Accomplished by Desperate Remedy.

Most of the evils which annoy manhood have their origin in youth. In that fertile and susceptible soil an enemy sows tares, which root out good grain and disappoint the harvesters.

When a sin would gain admission into youthful hearts and hands, it does not present its hideous and unsightly front before the face of him who shall become its victim. He would be appalled by the repulsive sight, and retreating within himself, would bar and bolt the avenues of his soul against the monster, which

> "To be hated needs but to be seen."

There is always some part of a sin bearing a faint resemblance to a feature of virtue which may be indicative of an ancient affiliation or fraternity. The sin may once have been a member of the beautiful household of the virtues; but, breaking away from the family restraints, it becomes the foster-child of Satan, coming forth into the world, after many years of pupilage, having only a very faint resemblance to indicate its relationship.

Sin is full of craftiness and wisdom, when she would insinuate herself into youthful hearts. She presents at first only those features which have traces of beauty, wherein she has her sole remaining resemblance to virtue. The victim is deceived by the specious appearance, and imagines that he admits the advances of the sin from admiration of the virtue to which it has resemblance.

When Satan determined to use human slavery as a snare in which to capture this new continent, that he might engulf its rising hopes beneath the desolating ocean, he did not use the knotted cables which subsequently bound us ignominiously in the dust. When first his net of bondage was thrown over us, it was light as the gossamer which stretches its airy length over the grassy spires of the meadow. It was not the slavery nor the slave-trade of 1860 in which he enlisted our unsuspecting forefathers. The latter was the legitimate but degenerate offspring of their mild and venial error.

The mild and benevolent Las Casas, a missionary among the Indians, first suggested the introduction of negro slaves into America. Indians had been reduced to slavery by the Spaniards, and were being rapidly exterminated by the labors and hardships to which they were subjected. Las Casas, in the kindness of his heart, pitied the "poor Indians," and proposed that Africans be used to supply their places. The suggestion was eagerly caught up, and an importation of slaves brought from Africa. The experiment proved fortunate for both dealers and masters, as one negro was found to be worth four Indians. The interests of commerce and agriculture being enlisted in favor of African slavery, its progress could not be stayed. In vain did the good Las Casas lament what he had done, and attempt to mend the mischief. He had "robbed Peter to pay Paul." As a priest of Rome, he would have been far from committing depredations upon any apostolic personage, and especially, however feloniously inclined, would he have withheld his hand from the "Greatest of the Apostles," the foundation of the Church, the antecedent of the Popes. However urgent Paul might be in demanding payment, every sentiment in his good Catholic heart would have hindered him from literally fulfilling the conditions of the proverb. How happy had it been for America, had he avoided the spirit as well as the letter!

We may very properly and innocently have

our preferences for particular races. We can not reject the testimony of our eyes when they tell us that one race is more highly endowed than another. In ordinary circumstances, in the retirement of our private lives, or even on the mole-hills of promotion which we reach in public career, there can be no harm in expressing admiration for a favorite race, and distaste for the uncomely qualities of a dissimilar people. If, however, we stood at a crisis in the world's history when an expression of our preferences would turn one of the great families of man into perpetual bondage, it were better to have the tongue cleave to the roof of the mouth than to commit the sin of uttering a syllable.

It was nearly a century after the mistake of Las Casas, about the time of the landing of the Pilgrims at Plymouth Rock, that a Dutch vessel landed a cargo of twenty African slaves at the village of Jamestown, in Virginia. Thus the evil of slavery spread from the Spanish provinces to the English settlements. Pandora's box was opened, and the brood of mischief was let loose upon the continent.

The slave-trade, being profitable, was encouraged by the mother country. Her capitalists embarked their fortunes in the enterprise, and realized rich returns. James II and Charles II were both stockholders in English slave-trading companies. The colonies remonstrated against the traffic by which slaves were introduced upon their soil; but the capital of England was enlisted, and she disregarded the wishes of her dependencies. At the date of the Revolution, 300,000 slaves had been brought to the colonies from Africa.

One of the acts of the Congress, which asserted our independence of Great Britain, declared the African slave-trade at an end. The infamous traffic was revived by act of 1788, and allowed a lease of life for twenty years. Our forefathers wished to indulge in the sweet and profitable sin a little longer, but declared, by solemn enactment, that after 1808 the African slave-trade should be considered piracy.

Slavery was legalized in states where it existed, with the expectation, however, of all by whose votes the deed was done, that it was only a thing of temporary expediency, and that soon the evil would be done away.

Evil, as well as good, has a reflex influence. It pays in kind. The measure a man metes is measured to him again. If a man sends forth a good deed to bless the world, it never wanders so far away, that it may not return to bless the doer, before he dies. An evil may be done in secret, and be hidden away where none but the perpetrator knows its place of burial; but it waits for no resurrection trumpet to bid it come forth from its concealment. In open day, attended by a long train of consequences, it goes to take up its abode with him who gave it birth, whether he live in wooden cottage or in marble hall. In the philosophy of the moral world, the angle of incidence always bears such relation to the angle of reflection, that when a good or evil is launched from a human hand, it never fails to strike the doer in its rebound. Those who violated the rights of the negro race, in reducing it to a state of bondage, did not fail to find that injury to themselves was close companion to the wrong they did to others, and that the two were destined to walk in parallel paths throughout a long career.

In the early history of the American Union, the votes which recognized slavery as an institution of the land seemed but the tying of silken cords, so lightly and so loosely knotted, as to be easily, and at any time, untied. By a well-established law, the cords grew stronger and more tightly drawn, until at last the nation found herself bound hand and foot.

Consequences the most unhappy soon ensued. The nation was retarded in her growth, and the expanding limbs were chafed. Mortification at length ensued, which spread with alarming rapidity, until many despaired of the sufferer's life.

Physicians were called in who promoted rather the progress than the cure of the disease. While the disease should continue, their services would be in demand; but with the accomplishment of cure, their skill would be no longer needed. Besides, having grown up by the side of the disorder, breathing its atmosphere from childhood, they had almost grown to regard disease as the normal condition, and so with easy consciences they indulged in the malpractice of prolonging the nation's disability.

In recent years there has been a great increase in the number of "Doctors of Laws." As supply seldom goes greatly in advance of demand, this multiplication of "LL.D.'s" may indicate increasing malady in the constitution and the laws.

It is conceded, among colleges and learned men, that the President of the United States should be a Doctor of Laws. Possessed of professional skill and prestige, he will be better able to feel the public pulse and promote the nation's health. .

As a violent and contagious disease seized upon

South Carolina in the time of Jackson's administration, Harvard University very wisely and patriotically created the hero of New Orleans a Doctor of Laws. The prompt and efficient prescription with which he checked the progress of the disorder proved him possessed of his title by better right than that by which many doctors hold diplomas.

Time produces great changes. The progress of years brings about beautiful compensations. The year 1859 saw South Carolina so far advanced in physical soundness and intellectual vigor as to possess a college capable of conferring a learned degree. This college corporation was possessed of such humane solicitude for the public weal as to cause our aged chief-magistrate, who had spent an ordinary lifetime with no title more euphonious or august than "Mr." or "Esq.," to be known in the world of politics and letters as *Dr.* Buchanan.

Every physician has his specialty—some form of disease which he welcomes to the onset, being sure that the result will render his professional laurels more umbrageous. A certain doctor, who prided himself on his success in treating "fits," always took pains to throw his patients into fits, feeling confident of their recovery when he got them into that form of disease in which his skill was always triumphantly successful.

Dr. Buchanan's purposes in employing his peculiar mode of treatment must be conjectured from his practice and its consequences. He was very efficient in producing "fits" in the body politic, but exceedingly unskillful in bringing his patient out of the epileptical and hysterical state.

Some of his subordinates had a taste for amputations, and labored hard to produce a condition in which the public voice would demand the "heroic practice" of dismemberment.

In 1860, when the disease had grown most desperate, the popular voice loudly and emphatically demanded a change of practice. Dr. Buchanan received notice that his services were no longer required. One of his subordinates was ambitious to be chosen his successor, but the people were unwilling, and signified their preference for an honest citizen, who had long lived apart from public life, and was unrecognized among the titled and distinguished. With diffidence he entered upon his arduous labors.

No human being ever undertook a great public trust with so little encouragement to expect success. The treasury was in bad condition; the navy was scattered in foreign seas; the national arms were in the hands of enemies. At this unhappy juncture, Abraham Lincoln entered upon the work of suppressing the rebellion, and restoring the Government to its old integrity.

When God's time and the nation's necessity had come, Abraham Lincoln sent forth his solemn proclamation by which a race of bondmen was disenthralled. So successful were all his plans for the deliverance of the nation, and so nearly universal the confidence in his fidelity, that, with voice as unanimous as possible in a country where sentiments are various and the expression of opinion free, he was continued in an office to which his administration was continually adding luster.

Just as the finishing blows were falling upon the rebellion, and his heart was devising a scheme of mercy for his enemies, he fell a victim to the malady against whose encroachments on the life of the Republic he had labored with so signal success. Abraham Lincoln surrendered his life as the last sacrifice in his country's cause.

The overthrow of the armies of the rebellion insured the radical removal of the great national malady, for the maintenance and extension of which the insurgent military force was organized. An amendment to the Constitution, having received the approval of the requisite number of states, and become the law of the land, has numbered slavery among the by-gone abuses which dominated over the unhappy past, but now are buried beyond the reach of resurrection.

CHAPTER XVII.

NERVOUSNESS—A MODERN MALADY WHICH BEFALLS THE MOTHER OF FIRST FAMILIES.

NERVOUSNESS is a disease possessed in copartnership by the body and the mind. It is exceedingly prevalent in modern times. So healthy were the nerves of our ancestors, and so unobtrusively did the nervous system perform its functions, that many of them never knew that they were possessed of the subtle threads which subserve sensitive and motory purposes. Some writers have asserted that nerves are a modern invention, like the steam-engine and the magnetic telegraph.

"We take no note of time but from its loss," so we scarcely recognize ourselves as possessed of nerves until they become disordered and diseased. Nervousness is a form of disability especially prevalent in modern times.

It is a disease more prevalent in appearance than in reality, from the fact that nervousness has become a kind of euphemism, or apologetic cloak under which to conceal unhappy traits and dispositions, or give them an appearance presentable in society. What was once distinctly called ill-nature is now known as " nervous irritability."

In ancient times, when fear took possession of a man and caused his knees to smite together, or induced him to perform extraordinary feats of agility in augmenting the distance between himself and a dangerous neighbor, he was called a "coward;" but now he is charitably described as " nervous."

Instances are not wanting in our national history in which our body politic has fallen into a state of "nervousness."

A few years ago, an old man with a score of associates made a sudden and unexpected visit to a village in the mountains of Virginia. The Mother of Presidents, grown old and nervous, became deeply and dangerously agitated. Symptoms of hysteria began to appear. Ominous tidings by telegraph aggravated the symptoms. A telegram informed her that a man had been seen crossing the Ohio River at Wheeling, with intentions apparently hostile to the Old Dominion. This news brought another shriek of terror from the despairing dame, who could only be quieted by assurances, from her chief public servant, that he would order out three thousand valiant men, who should defend her sacred soil. The telegraphic operator, having been misinformed in some important particulars concerning the passage of the Ohio, and wishing to relieve the hysterical lady, sends word that the person who had crossed the river was a negro, going not *toward*, but *from* Virginia. To render still further relief and set her fears entirely at rest, he kindly informed her that, as the negro had arrived in Canada, Virginia had nothing further to fear from him.

This well-meant act proved "the unkindest cut of all." The old lady was wounded in the tenderest part. Violence was done to her maternal instincts. Could she have believed that it would ever come to this, that her own children should be wanting in love, especially at such a time, and desert their poor old mother in this hour of her great extremity? The word which the blundering operator had put in with kindliest intent—namely, "*negro*"—sunk the deepest in her heart. The negro! how sincere had been her maternal affection for that child—and her love "passing the love of woman!" For none other of her children had she spent so many years of solicitude and anxiety; of none other had she so carefully calculated the value in dollars and cents; from none other had she expected greater revenues with which to prop her declining years; of none other had she more confidently boasted to her neighbors of the filial affection and cheerful obedience.

To be abandoned in such an hour by ungrateful offspring, is to have the poignant shaft of sorrow sunk deepest into the soul.

Jeremy Taylor gives a good illustration of the state of things in a case like this. That excellent and quaint divine declares the affection of parents for their children is like the mighty cataract, pouring its weight of waters over the precipice, while the return of love which children make to parents is like the mist which rises from the gulf below.

"Alas! alas!" sobs the terror-stricken and grief-dejected creature, "I have confided too much in the affection of my ungrateful children. My heart still yearns after them, though unthankful and unworthy. The man who has left me was worth a thousand dollars—perhaps fifteen hundred—as great a loss as if so much Virginia currency had been sunk in the sea. I fear others will follow the pernicious example, and I shall soon stand another "Niobe of nations."

"Alas! alas!" sighs the disconsolate dame, with thoughts of thrift and economy running like a thread of cotton through her grief; "alas! I fear his marketable value of a thousand or fifteen hundred dollars is not my only loss! How many years did he eat of my healthful hoe-cake and wear garments of 'Virginia cloth,' woven of tow grown on my own hills! How many times his own now worthless weight has he consumed of my far-famed and highly-flavored tobacco! All is lost upon one who has ungratefully gone to bestow his labors and his love upon strangers! Had he only gone to dwell among his mother's friends, I could endure the separation with better heart. I would also have something to show in his stead; something wherewith to solace myself in the bereavement. He would also dwell in a warmer climate, and have some one to protect him and oversee his interests. As it is, between Northern fanatics and Northern winters, I fear I shall never see the cheerful shadow of his face again!"

The infirm old lady hereupon falls back into the arms of attendants, in a state of nervous prostration. She has only strength, with "bated breath," to whisper her sanguinary decree, that all Abolitionists shall be hanged by the neck until they are dead, as a consequence of which,

"John Brown's body lies mouldering in the grave,
But his soul is marching on!"

So severe an attack of nervousness could not befall a single member without influence upon parts adjacent. The shock was so violent upon the Southern half of the body politic, already shattered by disease, that a stroke of paralysis was imminent. Indeed, for many years, the Southern arm of industry had been partially paralyzed. The foot had halted with a paralytic's limp along the high-road of progress. Nothing but the continually present strength and coöperation of the strong and healthy side could have carried the weak and trembling limbs of the South so high.

The nervous system of the Northern states has sometimes been wrought upon by groundless fears. Dread of Quakers and Anabaptists excited the New England Colonies in their infancy. Horror of witches filled the minds of New England's gray fathers, otherwise most sedate and self-contained. The impression which unaccountably gained currency, that such beings as witches could exist, was itself a strange spell of witchcraft.

Among the phantoms which for many years aroused our childish fears, the dread of a dissolution of the Union stalked tallest and darkest before our excited fancy. On many occasions had we thought ourselves in the hands of this bloody Polyphemus, who was about to tear us limb from limb. In those times of extremity we cried mightily for a season of respite, and frantically declared our willingness to yield everything, or compromise anything, that our symmetrical and mutually attached limbs might a little longer remain together.

Insane persons sometimes suppose themselves to be made of glass, and fear to make the slightest motion, lest their vitreous substance should be broken. A similar hypochondria seems at one time to have taken possession of the nation. She feared to take any decided steps and to make any great progressive movement, lest some accidental jar might render her worthless as a broken bottle.

In medical practice the galvanic battery is sometimes used with good effect upon nervous and paralytic patients. The batteries of rebellion brought to bear upon the body politic, with intent to produce dismemberment, had the contrary effect. The Republic, aroused from lethargy and divested of foolish fears, met the emergency with a strength and calmness which astonished all beholders. The vigorous effort gave strength and tone to disordered nerves, and restored health and soundness to the public mind.

CHAPTER XVIII.

THE MIND WHICH ANIMATES THE BODY POLITIC.

An ancient author wisely prayed that he might have a "sound mind in a sound body"—"*sana mens in sano corpore.*" This prayer comprehends a wide range of blessings, and in its answer includes immeasurable good.

The comprehensive blessing which the patriot wishes for himself, he desires no less ardently for his country. If a wise man, he prays for the health and soundness of his country more ardently than for her military glory and commercial greatness.

Our country has a frame possessing some resemblance to the body which individual souls inhabit. This body is of like passions with ourselves, since we, living and moving atoms, are its component parts.

To say that the nation has no soul, no vital principle, would be to take away its chief title to our love and admiration. We should see our country adorned with no attributes more respectable than those which the frogs of ancient fable beheld in their famous "King Log," and without treasonable criminality might hold it in similar contempt.

What is the precise nature of "the vital spark of heavenly flame" which glows within the human breast is an unfathomed mystery. Did we know the deep foundations of the individual soul, and its mode of existence, we might comprehend the public mind.

The soul of an individual man is more important, in many respects, than that which animates the nation. The former is a citizen of *two* worlds, the latter of but one. The former has attributes which shall lead it through all the hereafter, and render it coeval with eternity, while the latter has no element in its nature adapting it to localities, or periods beyond the boundaries of time.

Although the attribute of immortality gives to the individual soul a value which the commonwealth has not, yet emergencies sometimes arise when it is the duty of the patriot to sacrifice his life to prolong the existence of the state. The very fact that an individual soul is infinite in duration, while that of the state is finite, may furnish an additional motive, when duty calls a man to sacrifice his earthly life that the national existence may be prolonged. Once dead, a nation never has a resurrection morn, never hears a reanimating voice, while the individual looks forward to a heritage of eternal ages.

Although the state is a creature of this world, and destined to no life in any other sphere, its existence sustains an important relation to the happiness of millions. It is appropriately denominated the "Commonwealth," since the weal and wealth of every citizen is greatly dependent upon the perpetuity of a wisely regulated government. Millions might appropriately lay down their lives in battle, that surviving millions and unborn generations might enjoy the blessings of a government so good and great as ours.

Patriotism is a beautiful virtue, the crowning ornament of a noble character. There is, however, no virtue so pure and lovely that there may not be, lurking somewhere within it, a possibility which may grow up into a hideous sin or a monstrous folly. When patriotism grows into idolatry of country, it becomes a debasing sin. That patriotism is wrong-headed and perverse which would make a constitution more sacred than the Bible, and place the desultory enactments of wrangling representatives above the "Higher law."

Patriotism, being a virtue inculcated by the Bible, flourishes best under the genial sunshine of Christianity. The Christian patriot loves his country, notwithstanding some obvious imperfections, for he sees in its laws and constitution the wisdom of many great and God-directed men. He loves his country, for here is his home, here dwell his friends, and here his children are to inherit the legacy of liberty. His professions of patriotism are not made because he is handsomely paid, or expects to hold high political position as reward of his expenditure of breath. He is not so infatuated as to suppose that patriotism can perform the offices of other virtues, and write his passport to all worldly success and heavenly happiness.

Our public mind, like that of every well-regulated individual, consists of three departments—the Intellect, the Sensibilities, and the Will. Our sensibilities have the largest and fullest development. Intellect has not yet asserted the sway which it enjoys in mature and highly cultivated minds. We are not yet an intellectual people. We have been so fully occupied in building cities and creating new states, that we have of necessity devoted ourselves rather to action than reflection.

Like most youthful and immature minds, we delight in the excitements of sentiment and passion. As a people we delight to have our feelings aroused, and deem it a matter of no great importance whether the emotions excited are agreeable or otherwise. It is true that, "other things being equal," we would rather have the emotions produced by good news than by bad. The arrival of the "Great Eastern" would produce more welcome tidings than its wreck. News that the Atlantic telegraph is laid and in working order would produce more agreeable sensations than did the announcement that the enterprise had failed; yet we are always "glad to hear the news."

The doubtful compliment contained in the assertion of the existence of "an old head on young shoulders" has not been pronounced on the American Republic. Our public mind, though characterized by steady development, has not outgrown the body.

Our judgment is not yet mature. We are sometimes guilty of youthful rashness; we are prone to "let our angry passions rise." We are quick to take offense, and are by no means unready to resent an injury.

There is an amiable trait nearly allied to this which pertains to our national character. If our resentment is sudden and hot, we do not long retain the recollection of an injury; and when our first gush of wrath is over, we regret the hasty words and deeds in which we have indulged. We are prone to live by Cicero's noble principle: "My enmities are mortal; my friendships are eternal."

Our public mind has a quick and sprightly fancy, which infuses a pleasing liveliness through all our faculties, and relieves us of the sluggishness which some of our contemporaries possess. It has, however, led us into frequent errors. It has sometimes caused us to see and hear, where neither sound nor vision has had a real existence. It has sometimes beheld a new star in the heavens, which it has pursued with all the zeal of a new-born faith, and found at last that the fancied luminary was only the glowing emanation of an unwholesome marsh. No self-inspired and earth-commissioned prophet has arisen in our midst, to proclaim doctrines so absurd that they have not found enthusiastic welcome from us. No apostle has arisen with doctrines so whimsical and erratic that he has not found favor in our eyes, if he has put forward a specious argument in front of his fallacies. Carried away by first impulses, we are prone to act without reflection, and give the whole brood of monstrosities a passport to our hearts and homes.

Some nations, who had their origins in remote antiquity, permit Fancy to usurp the place of

Memory, and by her specious fictions fill up the intervals between the few and scattered facts which remain of early history. Thus sprang up the legends which amuse the readers of ancient annals.

The origin of our nation is so recent, and the printing-press has erected so many contemporary memorials along the path of our progress, that our history furnishes no place for the baseless fabrications of Fancy. Memory has undisputed sway over her own province. Few facts pertaining to our early national life have faded from memory. Some men still live whose personal recollections lead them back to the birthday of the nation. The storehouse of our national memory is occupied by great and soul-stirring deeds, which remain to promote patriotism and excite emulation in succeeding generations. From the facilities which the printing-press affords for fortifying this department of the public mind, it will remain unimpaired to the remotest period of our national life.

Our public mind derives its strength and energy from the people. No nation has a population more intelligent than the mass of native-born Americans. The great and responsible work of self government has developed the public mind and made it strong. The private citizen of America has political sagacity and general knowledge of national affairs, which in the Old World would be looked for only in a statesman.

In Europe may be seen stupendous peaks of intellect, which attract the admiration of distant nations by their loftiness and grandeur. Upon near approach, admiration for European mind is materially modified. The intervals between the great intellectual eminences consist of gloomy valleys and barren deserts. If the *savants* of Europe have reared their heads sublimely high, the masses lie profoundly low. The intellects of the common people have so little of the development and strength which results from self-dependence, that they readily submit to the dictation of any tyrant who may claim the right to impose intellectual or political chains upon them.

In the New World, if we have intellectual elevations less solitary and sublime, we have valleys less low and obscure. Our public mind has resemblance to the vast table-lands of the New World, which rise above the level of the sea, and stretch away for thousands of square miles, all available for the practical purposes of life.

CHAPTER XIX.

The National Will—Who may Express it, and of what Color they must be.

Polemical writers have written many learned dissertations on the human will. Many of these works have accomplished little more than to demonstrate the unanimity with which the minds of men are capable of forming the volition to leave them in neglect. The estimable writers have raised a sort of learned dust, which having, for a time, enshrouded their subjects, has at last settled so thickly on their books, that the epitaphs of the authors might be written therein with good prospect of permanence, from the extreme improbability that readers will ever disturb the deposit on the slumbering tomes.

However distasteful may be the Will, when served up abstractly, in a metaphysical treatise, there is nothing distasteful to a man in his own "sweet will." The process of giving it free way through the world is very agreeable to every man. So long as there is full liberty in this respect, he is on good terms with himself and all mankind.

So long as this liberty does not conflict with the moral law, nor interfere with the rights of others, it is the interest of all the world that it should be secured to every man. This great principle has but lately dawned upon the human mind, and has hitherto had but imperfect and partial application. It has had practical operation and effect only when the *ballot-box* has been the sacred receptacle of the free will of the people. He who would reach forth the arm of power to overawe the voter, or the hand of corruption to destroy his ballot, commits the highest crime against human liberty.

The ballot-box, in its simplicity and power, presents the highest exhibition of the moral sublime which the political world affords. Ballots drop therein as silently "as snow-flakes on the sod," yet they fall not so ineffectual and powerless to the ground. Like the avalanche loosened from the mountain-side, this united expression of the popular will overwhelms and buries all opposition.

The suffrage of the masses, striking thrones and dynasties, breaks them in pieces, and leaves them in fragments, to mark the upward career of the human race.

The term *suffrage* is derived from the ancient word meaning *fragment*, from the fact that in ancient Greece, where voting was invented, men wrote their will upon pieces of broken pottery, or shells, and cast them into a common heap, whence they were counted off, that the voice and choice of the majority might be known. Not only in view of the origin, but the effect of suffrage, is this etymology correct. The elective franchise, properly exercised, tends to reduce chains, crowns, and scepters to a fragmentary state.

It would be a happy thing if we could be true to etymology in political usage and practice in another particular. We use the word *candidate* to designate an individual who is set forward by himself, or his friends, as an applicant for the people's votes. This word is derived from an ancient word meaning white or pure, from the fact that persons asking for the votes of their fellow-citizens were vulgarly supposed to be possessed of purity of life and purpose. It was the custom of ancient candidates to array themselves in white robes, emblematical of that crystalline purity of character which they had, or to which they made pretension.

It is to be feared that modern candidates have so far forgotten etymological and moral fitness as to appear before the people destitute both of the symbol and the substance. Many of them are destitute of the purity of character which the fashion of another age was wont to require. It appears, also, that they have voted white robes inappropriate to the dust and soil of politics, and suitable only to be worn in another state of existence, after all worldly work is over. From the tortuous courses which they pursue, and the iniquitous practices in which many of them unhappily indulge, it is greatly to be feared that the end of earthly work will find them clad in the soiled garments of their worldly wear, with no provision for anything better in which to make appearance at the Heavenly Court.

The great question of the day, however, is not who shall be candidates, but who, as voters, shall decide the claims of aspirants for public favor. What qualifications shall fit a man to exercise the high function of sovereignty in the republic?

Age is an important qualification. The individual must have passed the guileless years of infancy—in other words, he must have reached the age of twenty-one. Under that age he is, in the language of the law, an "infant." This word means *not speaking*. The Shakspearean child,

> "Mewling and puking in its nurse's arms,"

is an infant proper, not having learned the use

of articulate sounds for the expression of its ideas. A person under twenty-one years of age has no voice nor vote in public affairs, and consequently is, in politics and law, an "infant."

Poets have plumed their most felicitous pens to describe the happy hours of infancy. There are elements in this felicity which they have never brought to light. A political infant is free from the perplexing cares which trouble persons who have passed their majority, concerning the party policy they shall sustain. He is away from the action and counteraction of those mighty motives which opposing candidates bring to bear upon the voter; each one designing, if possible, to secure possession of the entire man, and in the very probable event of his dismemberment, to carry off the largest share. Happy and care-free "infant!"

That he is denied access to the ballot-box may seem a sore affliction to young America, yet it is "a blessing in disguise"—a disability designed for his good—a means by which some years are secured in which the shoulders are free from the weight of empire, and the mind unburdened by the cares of politics.

There is, nevertheless, an indirect way in which young America has an important part in directing public policy; a mode which is by no means a new invention, since it was known to "young Greece." It was said, by an ancient writer on Grecian society, that the children ruled the mothers, who in their turn ruled the fathers—and thus the rod of empire was primarily in the hands of childhood.

Individuals or parties, when once possessed of power, are loth to surrender it, preferring rather to augment than to diminish their prerogative. We may be sure that youth has not lost any of its importance, or relinquished any of its influence. It is a "power behind the throne" which should not be overlooked by any one who would duly estimate the elements which make up our political system.

Another qualification of the voter is more recondite, requiring for its discovery and appreciation profound research into the depths of human anatomy and physiology.

The human skin is a compound integument, consisting of the cuticle or external part, and the true skin. The cuticle is very thin over all parts of the body, save the soles of the feet and the palms of the hands. It has no nerves of sensation, and may be cut or lacerated without pain. In this insignificant portion of the body, which is scarcely more a part of the man than his coat or his glove, there exists a coloring matter. In

Europeans it is nearly white, in American Indians it is red, and in Africans it is black.

Politicians, elevated to the dignity of lawmakers, being profound students of the anatomy and physiology of the human body, have discovered that the *rete mucosum* of a certain race is pervaded by a black pigment, and have had great violence done thereby to their refined and cultivated tastes! They have lifted up their hands in horror and indignation that any human being should be so perverse as to have his cuticle thus begrimed! They have felt rising in their hearts something which politicians call "pride of race." Like the Pharisees, they are thankful that they are not "as other men." Their cuticles abound in white pigment! Happy men! Favored possessors of the noblest traits of human nature! Their bodily surface reflects all the primary colors, and greets the eye of the beholder with white light, while the miserable African is so unhappy as to absorb all the rays, and—most unpardonable sin!—appears *black* to beholders!

"What an unreasonably selfish man is this negro!" exclaims the indignant politician. "There are seven primary colors: red, orange, yellow, green, blue, indigo, and violet. I skillfully combine them all in a beautiful bouquet of white, which I cast into the delighted eyes of all who look upon me; but this negro absorbs all the colors and conceals them somewhere in his pachydermatous surface, and refuses to reflect any for the benefit of beholders! Such perverseness deserves punishment! The obdurate negro should submit to the reformatory process of privation of political rights."

Our politician, being desirous of bolstering up his "pride of race," and securing to himself as far as possible the exclusive enjoyment of the privileges of citizenship, proceeds to dilate as learnedly as he can on the influence of color in causing mental inferiority, producing a "prognathous form of skull," an abnormal length of heel, and other ungraceful bodily peculiarities inconsistent with intelligent citizenship.

Persons who get their political gospel from politicians are carried away with the weight of such argumentation, and afford great instruction and delight to loungers about street-corners and bar-rooms, with their own deliveries in the same exclamatory strain. They all protest against being made "equal to a nigger."

"Be jabers!" cries an indignant specimen of a "superior race," "who wud a' thought that it's meself must come to this, that I must be considered the aqual of a nagur! It's meself that's come from Ireland only a year ago, and yet I enjoy the right of sufferin' for his riverince, the President of the United States, or any other man. And I would not think so much of putting a piece of paper in the votin' box, for niver a word that's on the paper I can rade meself, only it gits me such fine threatment from the gintlemen that's candidates, and I git so much good lakure to dhrink on 'lection day. No; St. Patrick save me from aver votin' for a man that's for degrading me to an aqual with the black-complected nagur!"

Another class of the American people has advanced a step beyond the position of our foreign born fellow-citizen, having gone so far as to say, that if pardoned rebels and traitors, whom we are now intrusting with the management of reconstructed States, shall prove recreant to the trust imposed in them, and again give evidence of a persistent purpose to destroy the Government, these liberal-minded citizens will at last overcome their scruples, and consent that the colored man shall step in, a second time, and save the country. They permitted him to become a soldier, as a last resort, when they found the rebellion could not be conquered without his help, and they are willing that he shall be the forlorn hope of the country at the ballot-box.

Rebels pushed the nation into the waves of anarchy and war, but the struggling victim, by superhuman exertions, has reached the shore, and is endeavoring to regain a foothold on the bank. Traitors, who almost accomplished her destruction, are permitted to stand in her way, and demonstrate their affectionate regard, by keeping her down, or assisting her to arise, as best subserves their whim. We make no secret, however, of our magnanimous mental reservation, that, if it becomes evident that the unaided efforts of the nation to save herself are unavailing, the negro, who stands near, shall have a chance to obey his patriotic impulse, and step in to rescue the struggling victim.

It is not in accordance with the great principles upon which our laws and institutions are founded, to make the right of suffrage depend upon a physical qualification, such as color. A far wiser and better limitation would be an intellectual one, by which a certain extent of mental attainment would be essential to the exercise of the highest rights of citizenship. It is unreasonable that a man should vote without having ability to read the name upon his ballot.

It would be no injustice to any, should the principle be adopted of allowing none to vote save persons twenty-one years of age, who are able to read and write. These arts are not so recondite that any man of ordinary capacity may not acquire them in a short time with little labor. The time and money spent in idleness and unnecessary indulgence, if properly employed, would enable untaught multitudes to master the occult arts of reading and chirography.

The application of the sovereign people to their books would have the effect to compel demagogues and politicians to take to their long-neglected studies, in order to fit themselves for the reception of the votes of more intelligent citizens than those by whose suffrages they have long been wont to live. Meanwhile the ballot-box will not suffer from neglect in the absence of these studious voters. The wheels of government will move more smoothly and noiselessly than ever, while politicians who have long held office by the favor of the ignorant are retired for a time to academic shades.

The adoption of such a qualification for the voter would allay the fears of nervous people who dread the consequences of Irish or negro suffrage, since the claims of the degraded and the ignorant will be held in abeyance until the proper qualification has been reached.

As universal intelligence is the chief cornerstone of a republic, such limitation of the right of suffrage would promote the stability of our government. The tendency would be to diffuse education, and make us the most intelligent nation on earth.

CHAPTER XX.

LEGISLATION—HOW THE POPULAR WILL, UTTERED AT THE BALLOT-BOX, BECOMES THE LAW.

THE ballot-box is our mouthpiece—its utterance is the public voice. Should it be destroyed, the people would be voiceless, and the public Will would have no peaceful mode of expression.

The lowest animals are entirely destitute of voice, or utter a wild and monotonous cry. Man alone possesses the simple and wonderful organism adapted to the utterance of articulate language.

A despotism is not endowed with means for giving utterance to the public voice. Not being possessed of the ballot-box as the organ of speech, the people are dumb. Their government being a monarchy, its voice is a harsh and unpleasant monotone.

Governments, endowed with human attributes, like those which give America her glory, have the organism of speech fully developed. They are endowed with the indispensable requisite to national humanity—the ballot.

Under such a government is never witnessed a spectacle, very frequent under a despotism, of

—— "citizens with terror dumb."

While republican people have free access to the ballot-box, no threats nor violence can strike them dumb.

Degraded nations without the ballot-box, and consequently voiceless, have yet some means remaining of expressing their disapprobation of those who trample them in the dust. They have it in their power to "bruise the heel" of despotic power with a mortal stroke.

Naturalists say that the serpent utters a hiss by passing air from its respiratory sacs through a chink constructed in its throat.

The chink through which the serpent hisses has no resemblance to the aperture of the ballot-box through which the public voice finds utterance. Men with serpentine propensities, with disposition to go prostrate in the dust, and eat that pulverulent substance for the gratification of Southern task-masters, endeavored by cunning and craftiness to cause the utterances of the ballot-box to sound like hisses of discouragement and disapprobation to loyal soldiers in their country's service, and plaudits of encouragement to rebels in arms against the Republic.

Their efforts were most desperate and most determined in the autumn of 1864, and never were labors more signally unavailing. The people never uttered through the ballot-box a purer, rounder, more sonorous voice in favor of human hopes and human liberty than in that memorable crisis of the nation's history.

Each individual voice consists of waves transmitted to the atmosphere by air driven from the lungs. Could the countless waves of sound, produced by thirty millions of free people, be gathered into one, it would agitate the earth's atmosphere to its loftiest hight, and reverberate around the globe with its mighty volume of sonorousness. It would be more sublime than the sound of many waters, and more harmonious than "harpers harping on their harps," as heard in heavenly vision.

Vox populi, vox Dei, "the voice of the people is the voice of God," says an ancient and erroneous proverb. Notwithstanding the irreverence of conceding to any number of men the attributes of Divinity, there are analogies between the voice of God and the utterance of combined humanity.

The voice of God is inaudible to mortal ears. The sublimest utterance of creation—"Let there be light"—awakened no reverberation in the silent valleys of this mundane sphere.

Thus the voice of the people through the ballot-box is never heard; it is felt and seen. It is a still—not small—voice. It is sublime and mighty in the accomplishment of what "man proposes" and "God disposes."

A voice of itself is of little moment, being simply pulsations of the atmosphere. It gathers all its value in its effects. It must find incarnation in deeds, in material results, before it can claim recognition among real things. A voice that is uttered and dies away without effect is mere

"Sound and fury, signifying nothing."

That utterance at the ballot-box, which does not assume form and shape in the laws and policy of the nation, is as fruitless of practical effect as Napoleon's command to the "head of the army" when he lay dying in St. Helena.

The voice of the people, as expressed at the ballot-box, unless it incarnate itself in written enactments, will have less effect upon mundane matters than the monotonous outcry of Bryant's "Water-fowls," as they utter their inquiring and answering "Cronk! cronk!" from one end of their wedge-shaped battalions to the other.

The will of the people will vanish, as evanescent as the summer cloud, unless it can enrobe itself in written statutes, and provide means for its proper administration among men.

The object of voting is not to indulge a childish passion for power. The sum and substance of the elective franchise, all it contains and all it means, is the selection of men to make and execute laws.

Jeremy Bentham says that law is an evil, because it is a restraint upon liberty. He asserts, moreover, that law is, like medicine, only a choice of evils.

According to this theory we choose men at the ballot-box to inflict the evil of legal enactment upon us, and make them our instruments in doing ourselves a wrong. The evil which men thus do, in gratifying the wishes of constituents, is not considered criminal, and the rewards received are generally regarded adequate to all the violence and injury done to the moral sensibilities.

Whatever may be the apparent evil inflicted on the individual, in curtailing his liberty so far as may be done by wise and wholesome laws, there is in it incalculable good to society at large. What each one loses of his own personal liberty is more than counterbalanced by his share in the common stock of security.

The principal evil in the "Acts" of law-makers of which complaint may reasonably be made, is their immense multiplication of works of legal learning, of which no living man has ever read the half.

Happy is it for the people, that these voluminous enactments are usually so well founded on the principles of common sense, that a man who never read a law-book in his life may be an obedient subject and a law-abiding citizen.

In choosing representatives to make their laws, people simply select secretaries to write down their dictation. Legislators have no power to enact a binding law in opposition to the people's will. No caprice of the politician can prevail over the silent but irresistible influence of public opinion. No legislation can escape that invincible power, that silent judgment of the people which corrects the mistakes of arbitrary legislation.

American citizens do not meet, and enact laws in mass conventions, as did the people in the early days of the Grecian and Roman Republics, and yet they take more immediate and effective part in making their laws than if they were personally present. Were the people present in one immense concourse, the pressure and tumult would drown all utterance and repress all reason. The works of agriculture, of commerce, and manufacture would remain undone while the people should indulge in the unproductive wrangling of the legislative mob.

Under the American Constitution we have a better way. While the citizen is honestly employed in his chosen calling, with all the dignity and independence of the sovereign that he is, he contributes his share to the formation of the public opinion which rules America.

Shallow men sometimes ridicule congressional speeches, by saying that they have no effect upon members; that the opinions of these astute politicians are already formed; that they do not hear nor give attention to what is spoken. They would further throw contempt upon such speeches by the assertion that they are made "for Buncombe," and are intended "for home consumption."

No intelligent congressional or legislative orator expects to move the politicians by whom he is immediately surrounded. He little cares to influence their minds or change their votes; for, if he should effect such a purpose, he knows he would accomplish as small a result as one who should expect to alter the direction of the wind by turning the weathercock, or moderate the rigors of wintry weather by warming the bulb of his thermometer.

The sensible and philosophical speech-maker in Congress addresses a greater and grander auditory than that which lounges, or reads, or writes in the desks around him. He speaks to hearers in farm-houses, in hamlets, and in cities. He directs his voice to dwellers on granite hills, fertile plains, and golden valleys. He addresses an audience not so fixed in error, nor so firmly grounded in the truth, that they can not be moved if sufficient motive is presented. He strives to move those by whose movement the earth is shaken—before whose breath politicians fly as chaff before the wind.

It is in vain for a statesman to try to legislate the people along the path of progress more rapidly than they can be conveyed by legitimate steps of national advancement. No law can elevate a nation to a high degree of refinement unless the people pass through the intervening steps.

The lawgiver who makes a law before the people are prepared for it, is the father of the most miserable of all abortions—a "dead letter." He stands alone when he expected to be surrounded by a willing and applauding people.

A friend of the freedmen, standing before two

thousand liberated slaves just from cotton-fields and rice-swamps, proposed three cheers for "Liberty." He waved his hat and shouted, "Hurrah!" but not another voice beside his own was heard. Nothing daunted, he repeated, "Hurrah!" and not a responsive sound was heard. Determined to see it through, he waved his hat and shouted a third "Hurrah!" but the freedmen stood looking toward him, with their great white eyes, wondering what it all could mean. It then, for the first time, occurred to the demonstrative friend of liberty that slavery was so cheerless and so drear a thing that its victims knew nothing of the meaning of a cheer.

Abraham Lincoln long had it in his heart, and almost on his lips, to utter the grandest cheer for liberty ever made or heard among mankind—the "Proclamation of Emancipation." He waited till the people were in readiness to join their shout with his. Many blamed him for delay, and called him slow; but, being well aware that his own solitary voice could only produce mortification to himself, and fail in the mighty moral and political effect which he desired to accomplish, he waited till the voice of the people, "like the sound of many waters," told him that the time had come. He then raised his hand and waved the Stars and Stripes as the signal for the mightiest and gladdest shout for "Liberty" that this world has ever heard.

Never before have the people had so great and good a lawgiver as Abraham Lincoln, because never before in the history of governments has there been a ruler so honestly determined to do the people's will. He was one of the people, and knew well the drift of their purposes; nevertheless he did not look into the depths of his own nature for the inspiration of his plans, but rather to God and the people.

These two are the "powers that be" in America. The One by omniscience, and the other by instinct, knew Abraham Lincoln to be the fit instrument for accomplishing the purposes necessary in making perfect the system of American government. Events produced such a conjuncture of "man's extremity" and "God's opportunity," that the American executive had the duty conferred upon it, under the war power, of acting the part of legislative, and by proclamation, the most sublime utterance of law, took the initiative steps in the most important statutory enactment of the world's history.

The people being the Moses, or actual lawmaker, and their representatives only the Aarons or spokesmen, if the former are intelligent and virtuous, it is not necessary that the latter should be possessed of great wisdom or extraordinary talent. Honesty of purpose in an American legislator is far more valuable to the people, whom he serves, than brilliancy of parts.

The majority of men sitting in our local legislatures and our National Congress have not been men of great learning, profound wisdom, or splendid talents; and yet our legislation has in the main been wise and useful. "Very small men get into office here," wrote a young man in the West to his father in the East, as an inducement to his emigration. All parts of the country are much alike in their proclivity to intrust the duty of legislation to the hands of men of moderate talents. Oxenstiern, the great Swedish statesman, said to his son, who was expressing his diffidence in undertaking a diplomatic mission, "You do not know, my son, with how little wisdom men are governed."

People standing afar off, and looking upon a career of successful statesmanship, are prone to regard the distinguished man of the hour with awe and veneration, amounting almost to adoration, forgetting that they are worshiping themselves in another form, and that the statesman is nothing who bears not the image and impress of the people who have made him.

Travelers on Alpine hights are often startled by gigantic specters, which appear before them amid the fogs and mists of that upper atmosphere. The specters which amaze them are but their own images reflected and enlarged by the concave mirror of the sky. The popular amazement at the figure and dimensions of a successful politician should be moderated by the thought that he owes all his greatness to his accurate reflection of the people's character and will.

Men have been divided in their opinions as to what is the true theory of legislation. Some have maintained that *utility* should be the rule by which to test the merits of a piece of legislation. Others have said that it should be tried by the unvarying and undeviating plummet of *right* and *truth*. Really the controversy has not much more practical importance than that which divided parties in Liliput, where the Big-endians broke their eggs at the large extremity, and the Small-endians avowed it as their policy to break them at the smaller end.

The great object is to break through the shell of formalities and restrictions, and reach that substance most wholesome and healthful to a free state—wise and judicious legislation. Whether this is reached through the instrumentality of utility, or eternal right, matters not, for man *can* not, and God *will* not separate these twain. However they may seem for the moment to point in different directions, when temporary disturbing causes are removed they will be found pointing toward the same steady and eternal star.

Ancient nations were unskilled in the theory and practice of legislation. Sometimes they were like children, utterly inexperienced and uninformed, and wholly distrusting themselves, gave the work of law-making into the hands of a single wise or mighty man—as Moses, Solon, or Lycurgus. Again, with the assurance and self-confidence of youth, they have claimed the right to do and say in their own persons all that was necessary in the work of legislation, as in the "fierce democracies" of early Greece and Rome. They evidently regarded legislation as something of small importance, and only to be indulged in as pastime in the intervals of war. The annals of ancient nations give the history of conquests with the utmost minuteness, and pass over the labors of legislation in almost utter silence.

Modern nations have the honor of inventing the art of legislating by representatives.

England and the United States have carried the theory and practice of legislation to the highest perfection. All other nations have fallen far behind them in their progress toward the attainment of that great source of national safety, happiness, and power—wise and honest legislation.

No nation has made so many political experiments as France. She has tried her hand at every form of government, and has tested the merits of every mode of legislation. During the Consulate and Empire the French had an assembly—*Corps Legislatif*—consisting of 300 persons, who were the most passive and tongue-tied company of law-makers that ever came together. They were not permitted to introduce or discuss a bill. It devolved upon the Tribunate to propose all measures, and to discuss them before the legislative body. This was a mere machine, set in motion and wrought upon by outside engineers. The members were permitted to vote upon the passage of laws, but this was all. As dumb puppets, they simply performed the motions communicated to them. Their votes were always in accordance with the wishes of their masters. Sufficient opposition was always allowed, to keep up a false appearance of fairness, and to flatter the people with the delusion that liberty still survived. England or America would not tolerate a mode of making laws by which the legislative body should vote, but make neither speech nor motion toward the enactment of a law. In these nations, the mass of power in the government is vested in the legislature. With them Parliament or Congress is the fountain-head of government, whence divergent streams of wise enactment flow to gladden and beautify the lands. Without the primary promulgations of Parliament and Congress, the Executive and Judiciary would sit idly on the chair, the woolsack, or the bench, powerless to perform useful duties for the state.

Our forefathers brought the seed of their legislative system from England. The germ planted in American soil, to which it was well adapted, grew more thriftily, and produced a grander and more beautiful tree than that of England.

The upper house of English Parliament consists of the nobles and bishops, while the lower house is composed of members selected from the younger nobility and gentry of the kingdom.

The colonies imitated the mother country in their houses of "Delegates," "Burgesses," and "Assemblies," and finally in the "Congress of the United States." Colonial legislation was very imperfect and infantile in its character.

The Continental Congress was the creature of a great emergency, and accomplished a magnificent purpose in our national life. It was a most remarkable combination of contrasts and contrarieties. While it held in its hands the most extraordinary powers with which a legislative body ever was endowed, it tottered along with certain points of weakness in its frame and constitution which cause us to wonder that it ever got through the long and weary years of revolution. While wielding the war power, and being the fountain of executive and judicial administration to the new nation, it was unable to control the very sinews of war. The Continental Congress had no power to raise money without the consent of the colonies. Any one of the thirteen communities, which formed the confederation, had the power to stay the progress of revolution, and cause Congress to sit as powerless as a crowd of school-boys. Happily the war pressure kept the colonies together. The doctrine which good Benjamin Franklin quietly and acutely taught them, that if they did not "hang together" they would surely "hang separately," caused them to stand closely under the legislative canopy of the Continental Congress until the storm of war was over.

When peace happily returned, and with it came liberty, purchased by sword and sacrifice, each of the colonies felt an inclination to go its own separate and individual way, and enjoy the fruits of victory.

Since the old articles of confederation were inadequate to bind the states into one great nation, with common interests and common destiny, a wise and good desire arose in the hearts of our forefathers " to form a more perfect union."

A convention of delegates from all the states assembled in 1787, which formed the Federal Constitution. The most important creation of this Constitution was the Congress of the United States, substantially as it exists to-day.

This repository of our legislative power consists of the Senate and House of Representatives. Theorists in statesmanship have been divided on the question, whether two houses or one are preferable, for doing the work of legislation for a government. The question is settled by the experience of nations.

We have noticed how the French, most self-sacrificing and philanthropic of nations, have made many expensive experiments in testing various political principles. As men go to old garrets to study the style and texture of worn-out garments or antiquated armor, so persons, curious concerning the character and workings of cast-off political theories, go to France, and never fail to find them.

The French, full of fine theories for a government which should surpass all others, merged all their legislative powers in a single house, which proved so rash and wrong-headed as to cause the nation to go whirling away through anarchy toward despotism.

The Americans, not so hasty as the French, prefer to "think twice before they speak" in the form of legislative enactments. Every "bill" must have three readings in each legislative chamber, and find approval in the sight of Representatives and Senators, before it is "entitled an act" possessing a form of sufficient dignity to command respect and exact obedience. Even then it is liable to have its career cut short by the veto of the President, which pronounces death upon such legislative enactments as are deemed incapable of becoming wise and useful laws. A bill so forlorn and unhappy as to meet Presidential disapproval has still a chance of "struggling into life." If Congressmen have sufficient regard for their hapless edict, which has been turned with disapproval from the door of the Executive mansion, they may give it a two-thirds vote, which entitles it to become a law without the approval of the President.

With two houses to scrutinize the doings of one another, and so much slowness of motion and deliberation, there is little danger that we shall suffer from ill-advised and hasty legislation.

The people are unwilling to intrust their will in the hands of Representatives longer than two years without renewal. The public is liable to a change of mind, and may need new Representatives to give expression to modified opinions, hence members of the lower house of Congress hold office for the term of two years.

Since we have no nobility from which to form our upper house of Congress, it was a problem with the framers of the Constitution how it could be constructed in such a way as to be somewhat removed from the influence of those sudden gusts of passion or impulse which sometimes pass over the populace. It seemed good to them that Senators should be elected by the legislatures of the states, and hold office for the term of six years.

"Old men for counsel" is a sound political maxim, which was reduced partially to practice when it was provided that Representatives in Congress must be twenty-five and Senators thirty years of age. Thus old they must be; how old they *may* be the Constitution does not declare. The only disability which can prevent any and every citizen, twenty-five or thirty years old, from going to Congress, is the lack of votes adequate to his election.

He who would know the details of our national legislation should read the "Annals of Congress," consisting of many ponderous octavos of political wisdom and forensic eloquence. He should proceed from these to the Congressional Globe, a series of volumes now grown so large, that he who should peruse them all would perform a feat well-nigh as great as that of Captain Cook, the first circumnavigator of our mundane globe.

CHAPTER XXI.

Executive—Qualifications Required in the Man who Carries out National Will.

The public Will may be wisely conceived, forcibly expressed, and plainly set forth in statutory enactments, yet if it goes not forth into action, it never has practical existence.

The people enact laws by representatives, and execute them by an agent whom they call President, selected in view of certain real or imaginary qualifications.

The American Executive must be a *man*. By this provision politicians are relieved of the active competition which would ensue were this office open to the ambition of the softer sex. At the same time we are deprived of those opportunities for the display of gallantry which Englishmen enjoy, as they gracefully yield to the mild sway of their good lady sovereign.

The President of the United States must be "a natural-born citizen of the United States;" a provision of our Constitution to which we respectfully call the attention of his Imperial

Majesty of France, who has recently manifested much interest in the American Continent, and a decided disposition to help those who can not help themselves, in the choice of their rulers.

A German magnate who should come to this country, with a letter of introduction written by Napoleon himself, and apply for election, by the people's votes, as an American President, would receive more bullets than ballots; and, if he survived to tell the tale, would have a sad account to give of the incorrigible character of the Federal Constitution.

The President must be a *single man*. It is not meant that he must be unblessed with a connubial consort. This erroneous interpretation doubtless influenced the "domestic policy" of a recent unhappy occupant of the Executive mansion, the melancholy close of whose political life may be due to his having no "partner of his joys and sharer of his sorrows." The American people are generally in favor of matrimony, and would rather have the "honors" of the White House done by the (proverbially) "beautiful and accomplished lady of the President" than to have the Executive mansion turned into a "Bachelor's Hall."

To be more explicit, the executive power of the United States can be intrusted to but *one man* at a time. Unity in the executive office secures promptness, decision, and force in the administration. Two executive heads of the government would cause division and distraction of counsels. If the men possessed equal genius and similar talents, the duplicate would be supernumerary, and serve only as a shadow to obscure the other's path. If the two possessed unequal genius and dissimilar talents, the shrewder man would be filled with arrogance, and the dullard would be consumed with jealousy.

The old Roman Republic was ruled by two consuls; and a most unhappy experience the people had of it. By way of compromise, it was agreed that each of the consuls should have the principal power in alternate months. As each one's taste of power was transitory, he endeavored to make the most of it. He walked the streets in a purple robe, preceded by twelve lictors, bearing bundles of rods and axes as emblems of authority. If any one was so unfortunate as to meet the monthly consul and his retinue, he was required to give way to him, uncover his head, and descend from his horse, if he happened to be riding. If any one neglected or refused these exhibitions of respect, the consul ordered the lictors to apply their rods, which they did with so much zeal and execution, that many an ancient republican felt that he was paying dearly the penalty of his disrespect for consular dignity. It was often difficult to decide the question, which of the two should first hold the chief authority. It was sometimes made to depend on which had the most children, or, if the number was equal, whose wife was living.

Although the Romans indulged in the luxury of electing two consuls at once, they found it to their interest to use but one at a time. These would have been very expensive indulgences had they required such salaries for their support as modern chief executives enjoy. Our sympathy with Roman tax-payers, amid the burdens of their dual consulate, is greatly modified by the authentic information that office-holders in Rome received no salaries!

The Romans were determined in their policy of having a double consulate by the erroneous impression, that one executive being an evil, another should be chosen to neutralize his influence.

The office of consul in the Roman Republic became much diminished in importance through division of its powers. Finally, under the Empire, Caligula conferred the office upon his horse.

The French, in making the experiments which

succeeded their Revolution, determining to profit by the experience of the Romans, and avoid their failure, chose three consuls instead of two.

Unfortunately for the success of the experiment, one of the three persons chosen as consul was an exceedingly selfish individual, who afterward figured quite largely in public affairs as one Napoleon Bonaparte. This triple consulate managed not only to perform executive duties for the French Republic, but contrived to do considerable of legislating on their own account. It was the privilege of the consuls to propose laws, of the tribunate to discuss them, and the *Corps Legislatif* to vote upon them. Bonaparte, being of an aspiring disposition, made tools of his two colleagues, and contrived to crowd the legislative calendar with bills promotive of his own personal aggrandizement. He had himself proclaimed First Consul for life, with power of naming his successor, and at length, casting off all modesty and all restraint, the consulate arranged and carried out a programme by which Napoleon became Emperor, and his associates Princes of the Empire.

Combination gives strength for carrying out schemes of corruption and intrigue, enabling an ambitious man cunningly to accomplish his ends by means of confederates, and avoid responsibility for measures which have in view the building up of individual power and fortune.

As republics are likely to become fashionable, and a great many nations are thinking of "making over" their old governments, or "mending them with new ones," some, in determining what mode of government is best, may suppose the Romans and the French to have erred in not having executives enough. Let them be warned by the experience of an ancient people, who submitted to the dominion of a number of rulers, who have some notoriety in history as "Thirty Tyrants." Not finding legitimate labors of statesmanship to occupy their time, they gave attention to certain arts, neither ornamental and useful, one of which is treated of by De Quincey in his learned essay on "Murder as a Fine Art." English etymology was a science entirely unknown in their day, which may account for their making the mistake of supposing "executive" and "executioner" to be synonymous words. These lamblike rulers were hospitably inclined, and thought to increase their popularity and diminish their enemies by giving "Tea Parties," to which they invited alike friends and foes. The fragrant leaf of China, which "cheers but not intoxicates," was unknown in Europe at that time; hence, as the best they could do, they regaled their guests on a decoction of hemlock, which had the effect to cause them to go off into a quiet slumber, from which they have not awaked to this day.

Some modern rulers have devoted their talents and their policy to the construction of highways, and other means of intercommunication, between various parts of their respective countries. It was the policy of the thirty tyrants to provide their subjects with free and speedy transportation to the Land of Shades.

In a "multitude of counselors there is safety," but in many consuls, many presidents, many kings, many tyrants, there is danger. When a nation gives itself into the hands of numerous executives, it will shortly need executors to administer upon its effects, for its days are almost numbered.

In a dangerous crisis of the nation's history, when responsibility is heavy, the individual intrusted with executive power would gladly divide his burden and place a portion of it on other shoulders. The nation, however, seems to take almost a cruel pleasure in standing off and seeing how nicely the weight is poised on a single man. They have a notion that the burden is better borne by a man when he knows that all the world sees it on his shoulders, than would be done could responsibility be passed from one to another by political legerdemain.

A man, knowing himself alone to be accountable to the people for the way in which executive duties are discharged, will use more exertions to show himself equal to great emergencies than if it were possible to share with others the responsibility.

There is somewhere to be seen a massive rock, so nicely poised upon a single point, that the hand of a man may cause it to vibrate, and yet the united strength of a thousand men would scarcely avail to prostrate it upon the earth. The executive power of America, poised upon a single point, readily yields to the lightest touch of the people; yet, so admirably is it balanced, and so well defined is its place in the Constitution and the laws, that civil war and foreign intrigues are unavailing for its overthrow.

In this country the responsibility of the executive is very considerable, and yet is not so crushing as to deter a multitude of aspirants from offering themselves as candidates for the office. The salary, the immense patronage, and the honor pertaining to the office are supposed to compensate for all executive labors and responsibilities.

While the President is held responsible for executive duties, he is not required to perform them all himself. He may call to his assistance statesmen of the best talent in the nation, who, as "secretaries" of the various departments, divide the chief executive duties among themselves. These in turn divide their labors among subordinates and clerks.

If the President were required to divide his loaf as well as his labors among so many, it would need miraculous enlargement and multiplication. As it is, the public bounty supplies loaves and fishes in such abundance, that the "multitude" is in no danger of famishing in the desert.

The sacred Scripture says that a nation is in woeful and pitiable condition when its king is a child. The Constitution has provided that this nation shall not be endangered by the indiscretions of executive juvenility. No one is eligible to the office of President under the age of thirty-five. We thankfully record the fact that no American ruler can die and leave us as a legacy to his degenerate and beardless offspring.

It is an uncomfortable condition for a partisan to be in a minority. He feels uneasy in such an attitude, and longs impatiently for that "tide in the affairs of men" that may place him among a majority.

A minority in a monarchy—which means that the king has not yet arrived at years of discretion—is an uncomfortable circumstance, which involves the entire population. In such an event there is a great struggle among ambitious nobles for the regency or guardianship of the infant king, for the care of his person includes control of his patrimony—the people.

When several natural-born citizens of eligible age, who have become notorious in military life, or in the tortuous paths of politics, have been selected as candidates by opposing parties, and placed upon platforms whose "planks" are mere

"Sound and fury, signifying nothing;"

when these opposing candidates have submitted some time to the contemptuous gaze of all idle lookers-on, and have been so covered with the grime and slime of slander and abuse that their friends scarcely know them; and when the people have been thoroughly instructed by the public prints that each and all of the candidates are more worthy of the gallows than any other worldly elevation—when all these consummations have been reached, the vast voting population go into the Presidential election.

In a simultaneous movement, though not "with one accord," the nation goes to the ballot-box. One state can not say to another, "Tell me your choice, and then you shall know mine." All must show their hands between the rising of the sun and the going down thereof on the self-same November day. There is no opportunity for an effective piece of party machinery, after having answered a useful purpose in one state, to go to another state and drag the people through the mire of political corruption.

By a strange freak of self-distrust, which is ingrafted by the people into the Constitution, they do not permit themselves to vote directly for President of the United States. The great stream of the popular volition is thought to be too turbulent, too much polluted by the soil through which it has flowed, to make it suitable to bear a man to so ethereal and sublime a place as the Presidency of the United States. It must be filtered through a "College of Electors" before it is sufficiently pure and classical to come in contact with the person of "the foremost man of all this world."

It so happens, by the intervention of so much machinery between the people and their choice, that the popular will does not always have its way in the election of President. The man who was riding most bravely on the highest waves of popular favor is substituted by somebody else in the secret channel of the electoral vote, and the people, standing by to see the grand emergence of their favorite, crowned with the umbrageous honors of the Presidency, are transfixed with blank amazement to see the glory given to another.

In no instance in our politics have electors voted contrary to the instructions of the states by which they have been chosen, yet it has sometimes happened that the majority in the "Electoral College" has not coincided with the majority of the people.

The electoral votes having been counted in the presence of the Senate and House of Representatives, and the result having been duly announced to the people, and to the recipient of the honor, on one blustering, windy day of March, in the presence of a great crowd in and about the east portico of the Capitol, the President takes the oath of office, swearing that he will "preserve, protect, and defend the Constitution of the United States."

It is surmised by some that there have been occupants of presidential position who, amid the meanderings of a tortuous official life of four years, have sometimes had but an indistinct remembrance of the fact and purport of the official oath.

The ancient King Crœsus was aware that he must die at last, and leave all his earthly grandeur, yet he found himself prone amid his royal pomp to be forgetful of the solemn fact. To fortify this weak point in his memory, he selected a slave, whose duty it was made to approach him at frequent intervals, and say, "Monarch, thou art mortal!" It would be well if our rulers would profit by this example, and employ a servant to say to them with frequency and force, "President, thou has taken an oath!"

We might borrow a useful custom from the Romans, if we have not already borrowed so largely that there is no prospect of our ever paying the accumulating debt. They had a usage requiring their chief executives not only to swear, on their entry into office, faithfully to discharge its duties, but also, on retiring from their positions, to make oath that they *had* honestly fulfilled their responsibilities. The prospect of such an oath, standing full and square in the path of the President, would present a mild solution of legal and moral suasion which would prove a powerful stimulus to the discharge of distasteful duty.

The Constitution made the executive power a reality, and not a mere abstraction, by constituting the President commander-in-chief of the army and navy. As Aaron and Hur, holding up the hands of Moses, caused the battle to go prosperously for the Israelites, so the army and the navy strengthen and uphold the hands of the President. It is a sword which is hidden in its scabbard in time of peace; but in war, wielded by an energetic arm and directed by an intelligent will, it deals blows with terrible effect. Few had an adequate idea of the tremendous power of an American President until war made bare the Executive arm.

The latest and most effectual mode of testing the power of the American Executive is as follows: First, exhaust the resources of brilliant tropical imaginations, and the vocabulary of several million voluble tongues, in heaping scurrilous abuse upon a newly-elected President; secondly, fire on the national flag, and set at defiance the laws of the "Federal despotism," fit out privateers to prey upon American commerce, and raise armies to maintain the heresy of secession; after all this, persons possessed of curiosity will be placed in position to know the extent of executive power in the hands of an honest President.

The power to "grant reprieves and pardons for offenses against the United States" is an attribute which presents the Executive in the most pleasing aspect, as viewed from Southern latitudes. Late Southern rebels find our executive tailor skillful in the construction of garments more efficient to hide criminality and shame than were the fig-leaf aprons of ancient time.

There is a considerable amount of political drudgery which the people do not wish to be troubled with. They are unwilling to be called from their farms and workshops to elect incumbents of all "offices of trust and profit" under the American Government. There are some offices for which they distrust their ability to choose worthy occupants. Wishing to save themselves trouble, they say to the President, "We have chosen you to the highest office within our gift; if you are the man we have taken you for, you are competent to act for us in the choice of a vast number of inferior officers, which we have neither time, inclination, nor ability to elect. We give you the power to make selections, reserving to ourselves only the privilege of bringing 'outside pressure' to bear upon you, and affixing the seal of senatorial confirmation to your commissions."

This "outside pressure," which is one of the "reserved rights" of the people, is a compound force, made up of the printing-press and the "press-gang" which crowds about the door of the Executive mansion upon the accession of each new incumbent.

Closely connected with the power of appointment, is the right of removal, which is vested in the President. "He can create and he can destroy." He alone has the power to perform the sanguinary work of official decapitation.

Official dignity conferred by the President is a "loose garment," borrowed for temporary purposes, which the lender is liable to demand at any time, thus leaving the unwilling individual to breast the storms of life with no protection but the homespun garb appropriate to private station.

It is not in the power of the President to unmake all the officers that his "sign-manual" has created. In the Judges of the Supreme Court he is the father of political posterity, which may survive many years after he has closed his official life. When he nominates the Chief-Justice he is creating an officer who may be called to preside in the Senate, when that body becomes a high Court of Impeachment, for the trial of the President himself, when accused by the House of Representatives.

Long occupancy of office is thought to unfit a man for the duties and demands of private station. Hawthorne, an old place-holder, says: "While a man leans on the mighty arm of the republic, his own proper strength departs from him. He loses the capability of self-support. If he possesses an unusual share of native energy, or the enervating magic of place do not operate too long upon him, his forfeited powers may be redeemable. The ejected officer—fortunate in the unkindly shove that sends him forth betimes to struggle amid a struggling world—may return to himself and become all that he has ever been. But this seldom happens. He usually keeps his ground just long enough for his own ruin, and is then thrust out, with sinews all unstrung, to totter along the difficult foot-path of life as he best may."

To avoid thus unfitting the occupant of the Presidential chair for the duties of private life, and to prevent the retention of so much talent too long from the great ocean of human activities, where it is constantly needed, the people made a constitutional provision that the President should hold office for the term of four years.

As the great question, frequently discussed in lyceums, "Whether the hope of reward is a greater incentive than the fear of punishment," is generally decided in the affirmative, the people were unwilling to deprive their Presidents of the motive to good conduct contained in a prospect of reëlection. They, consequently, say to their chief public servant, "Do your duty well, and serve the country faithfully, and if we deem it to our interest so to do, we will give you a second term of office."

This all sounds very well, and throws a pleasant atmosphere of anticipation about the responsible labors of official life. The best meant measures sometimes have an effect quite different from that which was intended. Sometimes motives in the machinery of life do not cease in their effects at the precise point where it was desired they should stop. Sometimes reëlection is the seventh heaven toward which all the virtue, all the piety, and all the activity of the President seem to tend. Under such circumstances, all the appointments are distributed with wise reference to the influence of grateful recipients upon November votes.

People are prone to impute a selfish motive, whether it exists or not. When the President pardons traitors, restores confiscated estates, or commissions rebels to public offices, people suspect that he is making provision for another official term!

European nations (their rulers rather) have expressed fears (hopes they mean) that the

American experiment of electing the Executive by popular vote would prove a failure. Their disordered imaginations have made the "noise and confusion" of popular elections intolerable to delicate sensibilities. They assert, with all the dogmatism of impracticable theorists, that our frequent changes and popular choice of rulers must be attended with extreme peril to the Government. It will be discovered, however, by those who take the trouble to explore the dark garrets whence European rulers gather their antiquated and cast-off political opinions, that their fears concerning the effect of our popular elections have more reference to the danger of their own governments than ours.

Our experience during the past seventy-five years induces us to suppose that the ballot-box is at least as safe and reliable a dependence in procuring good rulers as the "accident of birth."

No nation has ever been governed by a series of sixteen rulers among whom have appeared so few exceptional characters as in the noble line of American Presidents. Washington and Lincoln, the two extremes, one the hero of our war of Revolution, and the other of our war of Regeneration, stand forth as illustrious ornaments of human nature—men whose compeers are not found in any dynasty of history. Had our free institutions developed no other men of historic greatness, the fact that these were American statesmen would make our nation illustrious in the annals of the world. Both born on American soil, they never left their native shores, and never beheld the pomp and pride of European aristocracies. The characters of these great republican rulers were moulded among the people for whose benefit they lived.

Adams, Jefferson, Madison, Monroe, the second Adams, and Jackson have scarcely a parallel for talent and integrity among all the dynasties of Europe. The weakest and worst among our Presidents would have been regarded as models of virtue, in any of the Old World dynasties.

The English monarchy, in its long succession from the days of the Heptarchy to the present, makes a spectacle rather picturesque than beautiful. Alfred, the only one among them who wears the title "Great," was the noblest of British kings. Elizabeth was the greatest, as Victoria is the best of English monarchs. Cromwell was the only man of genius among them, and he arose to his place, not by ancestral right, but by force of his own and the people's will.

Henry VIII was morally a monster. His son Edward was a good boy, but a feeble king. Charles I was unscrupulous as a despot, and unskillful as a statesmen, possessing so little tact as to lose his head in the execution of his selfish schemes. James II was so wicked, and withal so weak, that his subjects, for a wonder, would endure him no longer, and called upon William of Orange, a good Dutchman, to come over and rule them. His reign was an improvement over anything the poor English had enjoyed for many years. His successors have, with few exceptions, been a motley crew of crazy, idiotic, or wicked kings. It is a wonder that mortal subjects would so long endure such follies as the royal race has brought upon England.

"There is scarcely an evil known to these countries," wrote Thomas Jefferson concerning European monarchies, "which may not be traced to their kings as its source. There is not a crowned head in Europe whose talents or merits would entitle him to be elected a vestryman by the people of any parish in America. No race of kings has ever presented above one man of common sense in twenty generations."

Twenty-three years afterward the same illustrious Democrat thus took off the crowned heads of Europe: "While in Europe I often amused myself with contemplating the characters of the then reigning sovereigns of Europe. Louis XVI was a fool of my own knowledge, and despite the answers made for him at his trial. The King of Spain was a fool, and of Naples the same. They passed their lives in hunting, and dispatched two couriers a week, one thousand miles, to let each other know what game they had killed the preceding days. The King of Sardinia was a fool. All these were Bourbons. The Queen of Portugal or Braganza was an idiot by nature; and so was the King of Denmark. The King of Prussia, successor to the great Frederick, was a mere boy in body as well as in mind. Gustavus of Sweden and Joseph of Austria were really crazy, and George of England, you know, was in a strait-jacket. And so endeth the book of kings, from all of whom the Lord deliver us!"

After seventy years of freedom under a nobler and more illustrious line of rulers, all true Americans are prepared to join him whose pen broke the festering link which bound us to the imbecile sovereigns of Europe, "to besiege the throne of Heaven with eternal prayers to extirpate from creation this class of human lions, tigers, and mammoths, called kings!"

CHAPTER XXII.

JUDICIARY—HOW WE INTERPRET OUR LAWS.

WE have traced analogies between the American Government and human nature. There is a point in which we reverently mark a high analogy with the Divine.

A perfect human government can have existence only as a trinity. The legislative, executive, and judicial elements interweave and combine their triple strands, to constitute the silken cords of government which bind American hearts and minds in a happy unity of life and destiny.

These three must exist in independent yet harmonious action, or liberty has no reality. When a single irresponsible power—whether consisting of one individual or of many—exercises legislative, executive, and judicial powers, a pure and simple despotism must ensue.

It is the great end of the Constitution properly to divide, adjust, and balance the powers of government. After provision for the legislative and executive departments, had no mode been devised for explaining and enforcing legal requirements, the political frame might have had most beautiful form and comeliness, yet it would have been in a state of suspended animation, and, for all practical purposes, would as well be dead.

The legislative and executive departments having been created by the Constitution, it was made their duty to originate that branch of government which should contain the judicial power. It was provided that this should be "vested in a Supreme Court, and such inferior courts as Congress might, from time to time, establish."

This power, being separated and ordained, was designed to run throughout the career of the Republic parallel with the legislative authority. No expectation was conceived that it would ever be absorbed in desert sands, or diverted into devious channels.

Although Congress was made the instrument in setting the judicial machinery in motion, it had no power to make its action cease.

As in ancient mythology, Jupiter rose in dominion above his father Saturn, so in the American system the judicial power sits in judgment on legislative acts, and decides whether they are in conformity with the Constitution.

It is not for the judicial power to decide whether a law is good or bad, and will have effects prosperous or adverse. The only question for the judiciary to determine is, whether a law is in conformity with the Constitution. This is the supreme law of the land, to which all departments of the Government must yield obedience. No executive power, legislative act, or judicial decision is able to alter or annul its binding precepts. The people alone have the right and power to change this law fundamental and supreme.

The Constitution can not be perfect, since it was made and adopted by imperfect people. It is important for the judiciary of the United States, as "defender of the Constitution," and the people as menders of the Constitution, to study well its meaning and its susceptibilities of improvement.

The rulers should consider the Constitution a sacred thing, not to be touched with hasty hands. It is our sacred ark, containing that which is most precious to us. He who rudely puts forth his hand to contravene its precepts should be smitten down by the people, notwithstanding his motives may be good; for. while it is the will of the people, it is the law to the rulers, and is the narrow strait which separates between us and despotism. There is no necessity that the people should feel an unreasonable awe of the Constitution, for it is their own will. With as much propriety might a man be afraid of his own shadow. That idolatry which constructs an image of wood or stone, and bows down before it, is not more mischievous or wrong than the idolatry which makes a formula of words, and declaring it perfect and unalterable, bends before it the knee of thoughtless and abject obedience.

Provision has been made for the amendment of the Constitution, giving the people means of improving our fundamental law, which should be frequently and wisely used. Happily for the stability of our Government, change of our Constitution is not a thing so light and easy that it may appear to a hare-brained politician in the visions of a night, and be carried by a hasty and unconsidered vote upon the morrow.

An amendment to the Constitution, before it can be considered a candidate for existence, must have the approval of the people expressed in a two-thirds vote of Congress. Then, having put on its best form and appearance, it makes a tour through the states, that the people may have an opportunity to see it in person, and express their approval or dislike. If three-fourths of the states give it their verdict of approval, it is regularly "articled" in the Constitution, and exacts obedience as sincere and true as if it had formed one of the original Seven.

Since the adoption of our Constitution great progress has been made in legal reform and in the science of government. At that time we took a position greatly in advance of all other nations. We are still in the lead, yet we have not advanced so rapidly as many of them have done. Having made one mighty stride in 1787, we have been satisfied to remain almost stationary ever since.

It is the old hare and tortoise race. The hare runs with great rapidity for a short time, and then, over-confident in his speed, lies down to sleep, expecting to awake in time to win the race. The tortoise jogs on with slow and steady gait, and passing quietly by his slumbering competitor, reaches the goal before him. The hare wakes up and rubs his eyes with wonder to find himself beaten in the race by a competitor so contemptible.

Unless we are careful to have our Constitution keep pace with the progress of the age, we shall some day be surprised to see nations, which we have long looked upon as hopelessly behind, leading us along the toilsome path of progress.

However much the Constitution may need improvement, the judiciary has no power to amend it. The judges must take it "as it is." If they wish to help in its amendment, they must put off the judge and assume the citizen.

As judges, their duty is to expound and enforce the Constitution, and test all acts emanating from the law-making power by its true and easy rule.

Their decision, "unconstitutional," is fatal to an ill-starred act of Congress, and gives it premature interment in the "tomb of the Capulets."

While it is true that the legislative and judicial departments of the Government are distinct, yet in a certain way the judges help to make the laws. Their decisions, on cases which come before them, have all the force and effect of law upon the judgments of their successors. In some cases the "precedents" seem to have more weight with occupants of the bench than moral, ceremonial, and statutory law combined. The most important practical questions of the present day are by them put to a vote of antiquity, and decided by a majority of men whose names have faded out of history, and whose minds never grasped the alphabet of the great measures which now absorb society. Such judges are so much the slaves of precedent, that the most momentous questions are finally and indubitably settled by a majority of one; and in cases of an equal balance of decisions, they scarcely trust themselves to give the casting vote.

The common law of England, adopted and continued in this country, is the work of judges, and not of legislators. Hundreds of years ago, lawyers adopted the practice of reporting the decisions of judges, and publishing them for the benefit of their contemporaries and successors. This work has gone on, through the assiduity of reporters, until now the volumes of English and American law number many thousands. Forty years ago, the learned Chancellor Kent pronounced the multiplication of such books a "grievance," and another distinguished expounder of the law declared it a "serious evil." Truly, the Chancellor's "grievance" has grown greater, and the "evil" become so "serious" as to furnish material for jokes.

The poor searcher after legal light finds himself groping amid the darkness of doubtful decisions, and bewildered amid a maze of labyrinthine lore.

Our neighbors who speak other tongues are as badly off as we. Nearly a hundred years ago, a French author, in his "*Lettres sur la Profession d'Avocat,*" published a catalogue of "select books for a lawyer's library," which he deemed "the most useful to possess and understand." This catalogue embraced two thousand volumes, many of which were ponderous folios!

The newspapers recently announced that a young American of respectable family and distinguished ancestry had gone to Paris to study law. It is to be hoped that his friends will interpose to save him, before he is utterly swallowed up and overwhelmed in the tremendous vortex.

One of the legal reforms which has recently attracted the attention of philanthropists is that of putting a limit to judicial legislation, in the multiplication of voluminous reports, and confining courts more closely to the statutes which emanate from legislative bodies.

Our Federal Judiciary consists of an "Ascending Series," beginning with United States Commissioner, continuing in District and Associate Justices, and culminating in the "Chief-Justice of the United States."

The jurisdiction of United States Courts extends to cases arising under the Constitution, treaties with foreign powers, and laws of the United States. Controversies between states come up for decision before the same tribunals. By this arrangement we avoid recourse to war, which is the supreme court to which independent states most frequently resort for settling their disputes.

When the nations of the earth become as sweet-spirited and as happily governed as they shall be in a certain "good time coming," there will be a Supreme Court kept up by the confederated governments of the world to settle national disputes. When that time, so long deferred, shall come, the military art, now so necessary to be known, shall be thrown aside as a useless study; in better words, "men shall learn war no more."

The states in their early history being "in limited circumstances," and many of them badly involved in debt, like individual debtors they had a horror of being sued, and a reasonable fear that, if their cases were capable of coming before bars of justice, they could not "keep the wolf from the door." Hence they fortified themselves by making an early amendment to the Constitution, providing that suits shall not be "commenced or prosecuted against one of the United States by citizens of another state." The consequence was that poor plaintiffs in search of justice, and debts due them at the hands of states, were dismissed from the courts without redress.

They had no recourse save "the last argument

of kings." But if the defendant states were weak, the plaintiff individuals were weaker, and an appeal to arms by them would have been as bootless as Don Quixote's campaign against windmills.

It is provided that judges of the Federal Courts shall hold office "during good behavior." The standard of "behavior" is not generally so high for the maintenance of honor in public office as is required for the retention of respectability in private station. Courtesy and custom often prefix the title "honorable" to the names of men whose individual and personal resources in the way of honor are very limited. The flattering title of "your excellency" is sometimes addressed to men who *excel* only in arts and practices which moralists do not approve.

Such being courtesy and custom in their bearings on public men, an office held "during good behavior" is usually retained till death. The bands which unite the judge to his position are more difficult to be sundered than matrimonial ties. Faithfully, and from his heart, he promises his place to hold and keep it "till death does them part."

Many serious and truthful words might be said in favor of a limited tenure of judicial office. It is a well-known phenomenon of human nature, that men greatly advanced in years are last to perceive and slowest to admit that mental infirmity has come upon them. A man who has sat an ordinary lifetime on the judicial bench has grown to feel himself almost an inseparable part thereof. He finds, the older he grows, his seat more comfortable and his emoluments more convenient, and fails to perceive the propriety of his spending the evening of his days in private life.

Our recent national crisis came upon us, most unfortunately, when the nation was under the dominion of an imbecile President and a Chief-Justice in the dotage which is the necessary attendant on the close of a life of nearly a hundred years.

The age of seventy years, being the period put to human life by Divine economy, should be made the constitutional terminus of judicial office. The years subsequent to three-score and ten, if Heaven graciously prolongs the life, should be sacred to preparation for the Great Tribunal. Some judicial functionaries have rendered decisions so atrocious and corrupt that they should have some time for repentance, and Pilate-like ablutions, or it will go hard with them at the bar of Him by whom judges are adjudged.

CHAPTER XXIII.

FROM JERUSALEM TO JERICHO—SCENES FROM OUR QUADRENNIAL ELECTIONS.

No highway has more unhappy associations than the road from the ancient capital of the Jews to the famous City of Palm-trees, whose walls once suffered so severely from the blasts of Hebraic rams'-horns. This road is perhaps not so celebrated for its natural features, although these are sufficiently rough and unattractive, as for the lawless characters that once infested its rocks and caves. To these the unprotected traveler paid compulsory tribute, without being allowed the benefit of conscientious scruples concerning the propriety of the payment.

Our country periodically passes through an ordeal which resembles the journey made celebrated in sacred history. Once in four years the perilous journey must be made. The nation scarcely recovers from the wounds and bruises of one expedition before she must go forth again to expose herself to the pains and perils of a journey to Jericho.

Being a conspicuous personage, none of her

acts can be private. It is impossible for her to go out on the most limited tour of travel, without creating as much sensation as ever attended a royal progress. Her journeys down to Jericho being made at regular intervals, all who desire to reap from them pecuniary or political profit have ample time to lay their plans and make their preparations.

Those who doubt the capacity of their own personal and private hands to hold as much spoil as their necessities demand, organize a band of followers, who are pledged to promote, by every possible means, the interests of their chief. There are always a large number of these petty chiefs, each one of whom is desperately resolved to outwit all others and appropriate the spoil to himself and his followers.

It is to the interest of these rival chiefs that the poor victim of their scheming should not be killed outright, for thus these skillful architects of their own fortunes would commit the folly of the unwise woman of ancient times, who killed the hen that laid the golden egg.

When there is such a number of rival chieftains, each bent on securing the utmost possible plunder for himself, without some compromise or understanding the unhappy victim would fall a prey to immediate death. To prevent this melancholy consequence, and to secure a continuance of their source of livelihood, a compromise is made. All who have expectation of securing spoil for themselves or for their friends assemble in "convention." Every chief, who sees but little chance of securing the lion's share for himself, subordinates his claims to those of some other leader, who, in consideration of this devotion to his interests, makes large promises, contingent upon the undoubted success of the great marauding expedition upon which the factions are united.

The "campaign" is now opened. A great deal of time, which had been better spent in idleness, is occupied by persons who possess tongues of infinite volubility in "darkening counsel by words without wisdom." A great amount of sparkling eloquence is brewed, which close inspection proves to be only froth. A great amount of muscle is employed in ungraceful gesticulation—directing attention to the stars, and pointing to East, West, North, and South—which would be used to better purpose in beating anvils or hoeing corn. A great deal of breath is expended, which, according to an ancient proverb, should be saved to reduce the temperature of "broth." Persons who thus bestow their breath have hope that the wind of oratory, having swelled the sails of their favorite candidate, may return after all to perform the above-named domestic service for them.

The day at length arrives when the long-anticipated journey to Jericho is made. An escort of servants and officials of various rank accompany the august personage on her "progress." They go ostensibly as a guard, but seldom fail to have their share of plunder before they abandon their "places of trust and profit" near the body politic.

The nation never fails to fall into the hands of one or another of the parties which beset her path. They do not advance upon their victim with the stealthy tread of a midnight robber. With loud shouting and tumultuous din, the leaders and their subordinates urge on their straggling followers. Partisan badges are conspicuously displayed. Banners are borne before them, inscribed with appropriate mottoes, conspicuous among which should be seen that comprehensive maxim which so truthfully expresses the great principle which underlies political parties: "*To the victors belong the spoils.*"

There is no necessity for minute description of the scenes pertaining to the great event which gives to every fourth year its importance in our political history. Victory is at length declared in favor of one or the other faction. The smoke of battle disappears, and the din of conflict dies away. Since it is almost a bloodless victory, those who took part in the conflict on the successful side survive to claim a share in the booty.

The quarters of the successful chieftain suffer siege. He gets no rest, day nor night, until he makes distribution of the spoil in accordance with the merits of his friends. . The few to whom have been assigned the larger and more splendid prizes go away with well-marked lines of satisfaction radiating their faces. Many depart with a style of speech upon their lips which is proverbially described as rather deep than loud. No booty can be so boundless, even though a great government is the victim, as to satisfy the demands of a rapacious multitude, every one of whom has cravings which extend beyond the boundaries of the possible.

Twenty-five or thirty years ago, the Government had a revenue so large that she paid all her debts, and possessed a surplus of several millions of dollars, which she kindly distributed among the several states. Her generosity proved well-nigh fatal to herself. Persons with evil hearts and hands corrupt saw this evidence of wealth, and resolved to turn it to their own advantage.

Since that time the country has seldom been

permitted to travel unmolested. Kind and considerate public servants have formed a system of relays along her route, and have always manifested great willingness to relieve her of her burdens. As gold and silver are particularly cumbersome baggage, and exceedingly difficult of transportation in large quantities, these zealous servants have manifested the utmost alacrity to lend their aid in lightening the burden. They have sometimes carried their disinterested patriotism so far as to relieve the country wholly and finally of all care concerning this troublesome luggage.

By a serio-comic use of the word "plunder," it is sometimes made synonymous with baggage. The enterprising emigrant carries his "plunder" in his wagon, and the honest traveler describes the contents of his valise by the same ambiguous term. Those who use this phraseology would not for a moment submit to the insinuation that they became possessed of their effects by other than the most lawful and honorable means.

The facility with which baggage could be transformed to "plunder," in the early and insecure states of society, may have first suggested the interchangeable use of the terms. The display of a deadly weapon, the brief summons to "deliver," and the small muscular movement involved in the passage of a purse from honest to dishonest hands, comprehended all the ceremony necessary to effect the important change. That which but an hour ago was the honest traveler's baggage may now be "plunder" in the hands of the bold highwayman.

There is no property of the Government committed to the hands of public servants for safekeeping which might not, without inaccuracy in the use of terms, be denominated "plunder." In this light it is regarded by many who aspire to positions of "trust and profit." Thus it might be truthfully designated by the statistician in his inventories of our national effects.

There are some actors in the scene who have not been noticed. They sustain the parts of priests and Levites. They see the poor body politic lying bruised and mangled by the wayside; yet, from their aversion to mingling in politics, they studiously pass by on the other side. They hear none of the piteous groans, nor do they see the ghastly wounds of the bleeding country.

They keep their religion and politics as carefully and widely apart as possible. Their arithmetic has a "rule of alligation" by which they arrive at the result that a mixture of politics and religion has not nearly so much value, in worldly markets, as either of these "simples" taken separately.

Many men will submit to hear pious teachings on Sunday, who would be unwilling to have an element so unaccommodating and unpopular mingled with their daily business.

When a church-going Congressman sits in his pew on Sunday, calmly calculating his chances at the next election, his attention is unpleasantly distracted, and his calculations disarranged, if anything is obtrusively said, in the pulpit, concerning the immorality of political sins. If he did not always contrive to have a Lethean stream—a river of forgetfulness—flow between Sunday and Monday, his equanimity would be disturbed, to the serious injury of his patriotic plans for the government of the country.

The practical effects of such preachings are seen not so much in the lives of the hearers as in the living of the honest preacher. He soon discovers considerable subtractions from the scanty sum which constitutes his livelihood. He finds, on computation, that he pays a larger sum for his freedom of speech than for all other social and political privileges.

This unhappy example causes some of the more prudent of the "priests and Levites" to make a large detour, when, in the direct prosecution of duty, they could not fail to see and remark upon the crippled condition of the body politic.

Other characters sometimes make their appearance in the scene. "Good Samaritans" often pass that way, whose humane efforts and kind contributions do much to prolong life and restore health to the miserable victims of rapacity.

The Sanitary and the Christian Commissions have been the Good Samaritans of the evil times on which the country has lately fallen. They have administered physical comforts to the body, and at the same time presented spiritual consolation to the soul. Their heavenly ministrations give us more cheerful views of humanity, and lead us to hope that the journey "from Jerusalem to Jericho" may erelong be relieved of its rough features, and become a safe and pleasant route.

CHAPTER XXIV.

How the Public Mind is Educated.

The English nation in its infancy was a rude, unlettered race, devoted to the battle and the chase, having more taste for bows and arrows than for books.

The Anglo-Saxons emigrating to England, like all early settlers, found much rough work to do. The Celtic owners of the soil were to be destroyed or driven away; the Picts and Scots, in the north, were to be held in check; that part of their sustenance which could not be procured from the chase must be extracted from the cold and sterile ground, by plows of sharpened limbs of trees, or other rude and unhandy implements.

The consequence was that our unhappy ancestors had little time for the perusal of books, had they been possessed of such intellectual treasures.

About one thousand years ago, Alfred became King o' England. He carried to the throne a marvelous amount of learning for that time. When Alfred was a boy, his excellent step-mother became possessed of an illuminated book, which she promised as a present to that one of the royal family who would first learn to read. Alfred's larger and older brothers found this literary eminence too difficult and dizzy, and abandoned the effort in despair. He persevered, and before he became king had actually learned to read.

Alfred became a distinguished patron of learning. He established a school where boys might learn to read, which was kept by a pious monk on the river Thames, near a place where cattle were accustomed to ford the stream, hence known in after-time as *Ox*ford. This school, having enlarged its buildings, increased its number of teachers, and extended its course of study, is now known as Oxford University, a fountain-head of learning for England and the world.

The monks, however, managed for many hundred years to keep most of the learning to themselves, locked up in the Greek and Latin languages, and consequently inaccessible to the masses of the people.

The mists and fogs of the dark ages clearing away, and the light of reformation dawning, learning was gradually diffused. The early part of the seventeenth century found the middle classes of England not very learned, yet liberated from the mental thralldom which had bound their fathers, willing to do that most difficult of all labors, think for themselves, and withal possessed of a most ardent thirst for knowledge.

A few of these, becoming founders of the northern colonies of America, brought with them all their newly-gained intellectual liberty and love of learning. They had no sooner erected temporary lodgings for their families, than they proceeded to build permanent and beautiful buildings for the education of their children.

Soon after the settlement of the New England Colonies, the foundation of a University was laid at Cambridge, which enjoys the distinction of being the chief seat of learning in America. This institution was located in the colony of Massachusetts Bay, and yet it received the fostering regard of the neighboring communities. The records of Plymouth Colony contain much proof of the esteem in which the new college was held by the people, albeit they were not fully initiated into the mysteries of the modern spelling-book. "To support and incurrage that nursary of learning att Harverd Colledge, in Cambridge in New England, from whence have through the blessings of God issued many worthy and vsefull persons for publique service in Church and Commonwealth," it was voted that "the Minnesters and Elders in each Towne stir up theire severall townes to contribute vnto this worthy work, be it in money or other guod pay."

The physical was made subordinate to the intellectual by the worthy Puritans, who determined that the very means of securing bodily food should be subservient to the mental aliment of the community. It was "ordered by the Court that the charge of the free schools shalbe defrayed out of the proffitts arising by the ffishing att the Cape."

The different sections of the country having been settled by separate and independent companies, there was no general system of education among the colonies. The progress of the different colonies in learning and intelligence was various and unequal.

Since the establishment of the Federal Union, the subject of education has been wholly given over by the General Government to the local legislatures. The several states have made very dissimilar progress in their provisions and appliances for the instruction of their people. Some states possess a universally diffused intelligence, while others have a population most unhappy in their ignorance. The world does not present two localities, under the same government, of more remarkable contrast in education, and consequently in every other element of progress, than Arkansas and New England.

Now, that the suicidal doctrine of States-rights has received a staggering blow at the hands of its own adherents, and bids fair soon to follow the example of error, and "die amid its worshipers," a system of universal education should be adopted by the General Government. Measures should be taken by which facilities for education shall be afforded free to all within the territorial limits of the United States.

The grant of public lands for school purposes, made by Congress to the states on their admission to the Union, was a great step in the right direction. Ohio, first-born daughter of the Union, had a birthday present bestowed upon her of a section of land in every township for purposes of education. States subsequently admitted have been treated with equal liberality.

A still more enlarged and elevated view of public interests induced Congress to give to Ohio, and other states as they successively passed the years of their minority, extensive tracts of the public domain for the establishment of colleges.

In the midst of the ingratitude and rebellion of the South, Congress generously and wisely resolved to distribute among the states that would accept the gift, many millions of acres of public land for the establishment of agricultural colleges.

As always happens among children who receive estates by heritage or gift from parents, there has been great variety in the uses made of their princely patrimony. Some have wasted their inheritance upon inefficient officers and greedy speculators, while a few have husbanded their grand resources, and now have a vast fund and a princely income with which to compass the glorious ends of universal education.

The recent grant of lands for agricultural colleges has been accepted by only a few of the states. Judging from the past, we must infer that many of the states will make little use of this magnificent gift, and, instead of wisely securing it for the benefit of all future generations, will allow it to be eaten up by the spoiled children of the present.

The General Government should take the cause of education more immediately into its own hands, and not do its work as now, in many instances, through the medium of distant and dilatory states.

There should be established in Washington a Department of Education, the head of which should be a member of the Cabinet, with a voice in the executive council of the nation. This great national interest, which has not even a "bureau" in one of the offices of Government, should be elevated to the rank in national affairs which its importance demands.

The bequest of a princely sum to the United States, by John Smithson, of England, for the establishment of an "Institution for the diffusion of useful knowledge among men," is an evidence that foreign philanthropists regard the American Government as a reliable almoner of intellectual bounties for the world, and is but a faint foreshadowing of the important trusts which would be confided to our national hands if we were ready to receive them.

This department should have control of the great national schools for the education of soldiers and seamen. The important influence exerted by these institutions, in the recent war, should cause us to control them in such a manner that they shall become the sources of strength to the body politic, rather than nurseries of state pride and hotbeds of rebellion.

In requiring a certain amount of education as a qualification for the voter, the Government would go far toward making intelligence universal in the land. However illiterate might be the foreign emigrant, he would be unwilling to turn his progeny out upon society disfranchised by their ignorance. This provision would secure the advantages of universal education, without the enactment of a law that every child should attend school a certain number of years. Our sons would as naturally pass through the instruction necessary to secure the suffrage qualification, as now they live through the years preceding the age of twenty-one.

CHAPTER XXV.

THE AMERICAN LANGUAGE—OUR GOOD HERITAGE, AND HOW WE USE IT.

Having a robust body and a good mind, nothing less than a great language is adequate to our wants. A mighty nation with a feeble tongue is like a full-grown man with the lisp and stammer of a child. Good laws, great commercial transactions, and glorious military achievements demand the medium of a strong and copious language. The languages of some of the great nations of antiquity are the marvels of modern times.

Its speech is the garb in which a nation lives at home and appears abroad, and if inadequate to national necessities, it makes the wearer ridiculous. When a language is built up by a nation, it is a true exponent of the character of its creator. When it is the heritage of a people, it has a great influence upon the nation's character and career.

The American people are the inheritors of a language made perfect for them by their fathers. They found it in admirable working order, well adapted to their wants. Its rough combinations had been harmonized by the labor of innumerable brains, which have long lain thoughtless among the clods. It was "licked into shape" by unnumbered tongues long silent in the dust.

The Declaration of Independence, the first utterance of our national life, was made in an impressive style of speech which no subsequent study and effort have been able to surpass.

The Anglo-American language is beyond all others adapted to the wants of a great and a free people. Being the result of a union of Anglo-Saxon and Norman-French, it has many synonymous words. There is scarcely an object or an idea which may not find expression on the American tongue by two different and equally expressive words. Our very speech, giving to us constantly the power of choice, is perpetually repeating to us the lesson of our liberty.

"E Pluribus Unum," our national motto, gives a complete history of our language. "E Pluribus"—"from many"—the Latin, the Greek, the Celtic, the Danish, the Saxon, the French, the English,—it is "Unum"—one—the ANGLO-AMERICAN. All civilized nations have contributed to the construction of the beautiful garb of American ideas, and yet it is not mere patchwork.

The combination forms a whole as beautiful

and perfect as the creation of an artist's taste. Its unity is as marked and as perfect as the shaft of Bunker Hill. It is the loftiest, most deeply laid, most majestic monument of the human mind.

Notwithstanding the vastness of their territory, the American people everywhere speak the same language. To one escaping from the dialects which swarm about his ears in a petty principality of Europe, the sameness of speech as spoken from Maine to California must appear most marvelous. An English word may travel to the cabin of the Western hunter, or to the utmost reach of American commerce, without losing any of its orthographical proportions or weight of meaning.

The American language is more nearly than all others a universal tongue. It is spoken on every sea, and is echoed by every shore. An American can scarcely be cast on a shore so desolate and uncultivated that his words will not fall upon understanding ears. To the old English question, "Who reads an American book?" it may now be answered, "Everybody," and that omnipresent personage has taken pains to learn the language, that he may enjoy the privilege.

It is a better fortune than wealth or noble birth to be born to the inheritance of such a language as our mother tongue. It enables us to give full utterance to our thoughts in the ears of the only free people on earth. It enables us to address heart-moving motives to the only men on earth who dare to allow words to have their full influence.

He who can marshal English words and phrases in such a way as to capture the human mind, either by stratagem or by storm, has greater power than the barbaric despot whose commands are carried out by armies of obedient slaves.

The English language presents to him whose mother tongue it is, a more valuable material for intellectual labors than the ancient artist had in quarries of Parian marble. In this material Shakspeare and Milton wrought, and reared their monuments. There are many languages widely spoken in the world, in which it would be as fruitless to attempt to create a great intellectual work as to build enduring pyramids of Nile mud or frost-work.

Happy is the man who thinks his thoughts and speaks his words in the English tongue. Happy is he who can read Shakspeare, and Milton, and King James' Bible without translation. Wretched is he who must plod through foreign grammars, and wear out ponderous dictionaries, which he never fully masters, that he may gain a smattering of English. Thrice wretched is he who toils through a tedious lifetime without knowing a word of the American language. The only mitigation of his misery is that he knows not its extent. Like the man who gropes through a cave of diamonds in the dark, he lives and dies without knowing the existence of the treasures he has failed to appropriate and possess.

Our language has been the medium of great intellectual power and influence. Thoughts are enshrined therein which will have authority in remotest ages.

The American language is the most effective medium of political power in the world. A speech in Congress on some momentous question of the times has an audience of millions. In no other language than ours would the Proclamation of Emancipation have thrilled the world with so deep an interest.

Grammatical and rhetorical accuracy is characteristic of our nation. Writers of English undefiled are universally read in America, and acknowledged as authority in modes of expression. Every school-boy knows where to find the law and the testimony in all matters of orthography, pronunciation, and definition.

We are correct in our speech, from the fact that

we are so much a traveling people. No American imagines

"The visual line that girds him round, the world's extreme."

Every one has traveled to other portions of the country, and has conversed with people who have their habitation outside his native vale. The native of New England, of Pennsylvania, and North Carolina have moved West, and settled on adjoining farms. If one carries with him a provincialism in his speech, the good-humored laugh of his neighbors soon dissipates it, and the language of the pioneer neighborhood becomes classically pure.

The little curious provincialisms which arise from obscure fountains are lost in the great aggregate of pure speech. The ocean is the receptacle of impurities from every shore, but its agitation by tides and storms gives the mighty mass its purity and grandeur.

The moral character of a nation may be determined by listening to its speech. Out of its own mouth must a nation as well as an individual be judged.

One of our faults in speech, which in its incipiency is ridiculous, but in its progress and perfection becomes immoral, is our tendency to exaggeration. We appear to our visitors from abroad as a nation of boasters. We grow hyperbolical on the smallest provocation. All our emotions are "overwhelming." Our scenery is "splendid," "magnificent," "awful." Our origin is "wonderful," our progress "sublime," our future "glorious." Our birth was an "era," our history is an "epic;" our end, if it ever comes, will be the greatest "tragedy" ever performed. We are the greatest commercial, intellectual, and military nation on the globe. We could vanquish all Europe, perhaps the combined world, on the field of battle.

All parts of our country are not equally given to boasting. In this art the South has always excelled. Some of the exaggerations of Southern people have led them into most unhappy consequences. It was asserted by ardent declaimers that "one Southern man could whip five Yankees." The people of the North were either too busy or too taciturn to refute the falsehood, and so its perpetrators began to consider it unimpeachably true. They founded all their arithmetic on it, and made their preparations for war on this basis. Every Southerner who enlisted under the rebel flag imagined himself another Goliath of Gath, commissioned to defy the cowardly armies of the North.

Every school-boy has read the story of the

unhappy man who wrecked his fortunes and his mind by making the little numerical mistake of saying, "Once one is two." This refrain was on his tongue through all his future life: "Once one is two;" "once one is two." When corrected, he would seem to collect his shattered thoughts and say, "Ah! right; once one is one," and then his unsphered mind would revert to its old error, and continue to repeat, "Once one is two."

The South lost its political and material wealth by making the foolish mistake of computing "*one* equal to five." This little mistake on the Southern slate has been wiped out in blood. The erring accountant has learned a lesson, and will henceforth work by a better rule.

Our language is not trivial nor low; it is elevated and dignified in its character, as is natural from its origin with the earnest and solemn Saxons. It is appropriate and adapted to the uses and purposes of every-day life, from its use by the most practical nation on earth. It is pure, it is chaste, it is religious; otherwise it could not have crossed the Atlantic with Puritans and Quakers. It possesses, what some languages have not, words with which to name the Deity, describe his attributes, and define the doctrines of his Word.

We have words by which he who studies to be

vile may give expression to thoughts vulgar and profane. Such words are ill at ease; they are not at home among us. They mar the harmony of English periods. They can not well flow in the current of smooth and quiet thought. They only appear amid the turbulence of passion. A Frenchman can make his profanity coalesce with his speech so smoothly that one hardly notices its presence. He swears with his politest bow; he swears in the midst of his gayest humor. He wreathes his oath with smiles, and utters it with such affability that the heedless hearer scarcely thinks that it needs apology.

On the other hand, the circumstances under which an American uses an oath make it abhorrent to the taste as well as the moral sensibility. It is rarely used save as the vehicle of his anger or impatience. It is the impotent attempt of a passionate man to do by word what he can not or dare not do in deed. In this uncouth manner he "eases his mind," or "does justice to a subject." When the profane man has made the moral and mental atmosphere murky with his oaths, and pauses to take breath, he perceives that his furious language has not changed the physical relations of anything about him. He has not made one hair white or black.

We have never heard of any physical effects

produced by profanity, unless we credit the averment of mule-drivers in military service. They affirm (if a term so mild and Quakerlike can be predicated of men who constantly swear,) that their obdurate and stubborn beasts absolutely refused to extract loaded wagons from Southern mud until the drivers began to curse. According to these authorities, profanity is the only language which these animals can comprehend. It is no flattery to men who use such language, that their habitual speech is not above the level of brute comprehension.

These poor beasts are grossly slandered by those who aver that they have any liking for such language. If the statements of their drivers are true, they only prove the fact that the taste and disposition of the poor animals induced them to do all they could to put an end to their proximity to persons who indulged in such wicked speech. It was hard that the strength of harness and weight of load often prevented the accomplishment of their laudable desires.

Those who declare that mules have any sympathy with men profane do injustice to the brute creation, as did those who reported to an American General that one of his subordinate officers had been "beastly drunk." In his order dismissing the offender from the service, the General vindicated the honor of slandered animals, by saying that "beasts never get drunk."

Some who have denied the doctrine of a hell as a place for the future punishment of the wicked, confess themselves convinced by the Southern rebellion that such a place is necessary, and does certainly exist, or the universe is sadly incomplete. This life, they think, is inadequate for the just punishment of such sinners, and there is no place suitable for their consignment in the life to come, save the place revealed in Scripture as prepared for the first rebels, "the devil and his angels."

It is to be feared that some have concluded that there is a use for profane language in its application to the character and crimes of rebels. They think that the unparalleled wickedness and folly of these miscreants will justify the most opprobrious and profane epithets that can be heaped upon them. It must be admitted that there is temptation to intemperate language in the vain attempt to describe such unparalleled crimes. They have overleaped all the barriers which divine and human law reared against wickedness. This, however, gives no license for breach of morals or propriety by those whose minds are well disposed.

The angel, whose office as God's especial messenger would have given him right to the utterance of fiercest denunciations, set limits to his speech, on a most trying occasion, when he brought no "railing accusation" against Satan, but left him in the hands of God for judgment and condemnation. Satan's servants and imitators may safely be left to the pains and penalties provided by human and divine laws, both of which they have trampled under foot.

There is danger of our becoming a nation of oath-makers, and consequently of oath-breakers. He who asseverates by the Supreme Being on every trivial occasion can have little reverence for His name when used in courts of justice. Frequent perjury is a natural result of widespread profanity. It is not more important to ask a witness whether he believes in God, before administering an oath, than whether he habitually uses His name profanely. The testimony of a profane swearer should have little weight when it is at variance with the evidence of one who has due reverence for God.

The public conscience and the public taste should combine to save our Anglo-American tongue from corruption. Melancholy would be our condition, should increasing profanity not speedily be stayed. All classes and ages would soon be infected by the deadly virus. We should be shocked everywhere by sounds most harsh and discordant. The child would lisp profanity, and the man of age would utter blasphemies against the Being in whose presence he must shortly stand. Such untimely sinning would indicate a depravity of the public heart almost beyond the reach of remedy.

CHAPTER XXVI.

THE PUBLIC PIETY—DIFFERENCE BETWEEN A RELIGIOUS STATE AND A STATE RELIGION.

Man has been called a religious animal, yet in some of his phases many of the lower orders of creation are quite as worthy of commendation for piety as himself.

Man has high motives to religious life, since he has an immortal soul derived from God, and bears in his breast a moral principle which all along the career of life condemns or acquits, as a court subordinate to the Divine Bar.

The Body Politic—the State—can have no religion. It is the creation of man, and, like all his works, is finite. It moves in slow and stately march through the centuries toward the end of its existence; and possessing a mortal soul, it can have no renewal of life beyond the shores of time.

State religion is a mere idea, which can have no truthful and tangible existence. God should be recognized and honored in national constitutions; but this is merely an admission that men are not and can not be Atheists.

In Him nations "live and move and have their being," and they can no more ignore His existence than they can call in question the shining of the sun, or the presence of the all-pervading atmosphere.

The Bible must be the basis of all correct legislation, since it embodies the first principles of jurisprudence. No human assembly can legislate into existence a principle of law which has not its origin in the Sacred Code.

When rulers attempt to create religion for the state, they go beyond their province. They produce a creation for which the nationality has no need, and in which it can take no interest. The consequence is that it dies as soon as born, and if nurtured at all, it is only a piece of coldness and corruption in the nation's arms. The living human being derives its first inspiration by gift of Heaven, and ever afterward, until the wheels of life stand still, the vital air comes and goes of its own accord amid the pulmonary cells. The wooden man, the mere machine, may be inflated for a moment with fictitious breath; but it has no vitalizing effects, and can only be continued by the constant renewal of the external force. The state is but a constructive man, a piece of human machinery, and no religion better than a mere form, a shadow, is adapted to it. The legislation which constructs the ropes and pulleys must supply the motive power.

The English are so unhappy as to have a state religion. Like their monarchy, it is a mockery. The two go well together, as the one absurdity serves to bolster up the other. The establishment flourishes beneath the smiles of royalty, and the Church, by way of compensation, keeps monarchy in good repute, singing, in her sublime devotions, "God save the Queen," and praying most fervently, "God grant her in health and wealth long to live."

The Church of England, being a parasite of the state, is not deep-rooted among the everlasting hills of God, but draws all its vitality from the political system from which it derives its origin. The establishment derives great revenue from its unhappy relation to the state, the only legitimate effect of which is to make the bishops immensely rich, and render the inferior clergy and the wretched people more abject.

Formalism and Hypocrisy run riot in the established Church. The greater portion of English piety has taken refuge among the non-conforming sects. The people groan under an oppression which compels them to pay enormous taxes to support a non-resident and slothful clergy. After this if they would see the pastors of their choice enjoy a meager livelihood, they must divide with them the scanty remainder in voluntary contributions.

Americans have reason to be thankful that God in his mercy has saved them from two stupendous evils: the delusion of bowing down to dumb idols, and the burden of bearing a national Church.

Happily for us, when the American Colonies were established, the policy of the English Church was to oppress Puritans, Catholics, and Quakers. The consequence was that these incorrigible schismatics and sectaries brought with them no admiration for the established Church. They were in no danger of attempting any feeble imitations of English hierarchy in the New World. The colonists announced the broad principle, without which civil liberty is a mockery, that no man should suffer disability as a citizen on account of his religious belief.

So thoroughly was the American public mind persuaded of the evils of a united Church and State, that the first amendment made simultaneously with the adoption of the Constitution provided that "Congress shall make no law respecting an establishment of religion, or prohibiting the free exercise thereof." Thus our vast territory became a field for the emulation of the religious sects and the exercise of their pious zeal. Happily the ambition to become an established Church can not exist among the aspirations and rivalries of the sects. A prize so blighting to the state and so fatal to the Churches does not exist among their possible temptations.

Honest and God-fearing rulers are inestimable blessings to the state. Their piety, however, should be the real outgrowth of a faith deeply rooted in their hearts, and their tenure of office the consequence of the people's choice. Hence it was wisely enacted in the Constitution that "No religious test shall ever be required as a qualification to any office or public trust under the United States."

To the hypocritical monarchies of the Old World, whose statutes are loaded with the ordinances of an effete formalism, we may appear to be an irreligious, an infidel people, and yet, destitute as we are of legal enactments to enforce religion, we are, without hypocrisy, the most religious nation on the globe.

The American nation had its foundation in the aspirations of pure Christianity, seeking free and full development. The early emigrants from England to America were not ambitious to extend the boundaries of the British Empire

They cared not to be able to boast that "the sun never sets on British dominions."

They were desirous to extend the conquests of another kingdom—the kingdom of Christ. They did not embark, like the Spanish adventurers, to seek the gold of Mexico or Peru. They were content to find a place where they would gain but a scanty livelihood on earth, so that they might have an opportunity to lay up treasures in heaven.

They built on the shores of the New World no baronial castles, no royal palaces; they reared a nobler and grander fabric—the glorious temple of American liberty, having for its firm and deep foundations the eternal principles of Christianity.

The Puritans of New England, the Catholics of Maryland, the Baptists of Rhode Island, and the Quakers of Pennsylvania had all suffered too much at the hands of a national Church to think of fastening such an incumbrance on the new settlements of America. They had sacrificed too much for conscience' sake, and for religion's sake, not to make Christianity an essential element in their new institutions.

Escaping the calamity of a state religion, we have inherited from our fathers a religious state. In the dark hours of revolutionary trial we were sustained by a "firm reliance on Almighty God." Our fathers had faith in God. They well knew that vain would be reliance on their limited resources and untrained militia against the vast armaments and practiced soldiery of Europe, unless Divinity should "shape their ends."

The Continental Congress, in whose hands were intrusted the highest and best destinies of the human race, called upon God to direct their momentous deliberations. He guided them to the choice of Washington to be commander-in-chief.

Faith in God and devotion to the cause of liberty did more for him and his country, than faith in his destiny and devotion to himself did for Napoleon Bonaparte and for France. Napoleon's maxim was, that God was on the side which had the heaviest battalions; but he outlived all his military success and imperial grandeur, and perished a miserable exile on an ocean rock. Washington believed that God was on the side of the few and the feeble, struggling faithfully for human rights. He brought to a triumphant close the most hopeless and unequal struggle that the world has ever seen. He gave to the American people liberties unimpaired by his own ambition. By his example he made it high treason against humanity for one of his successors to abate a jot of our heritage of freedom.

Since the days of Washington there have sometimes been men in authority among us who have "feared not God nor regarded man." Aaron Burr could plot the dismemberment of the Union, and the establishment of a Western Empire; Calhoun could deliberately and wickedly design the secession of the South, which he was too feeble to accomplish; Taney, our "atrocious Judge," could turn Justice aside from her high and holy course, and cause her garments to be defiled by prostration before the "sum of all villainies;" Buchanan could wickedly and weakly sit in the executive chair, and see, without an effort to prevent them, deeds of high-handed robbery and treason committed in the inner shrine of the Temple of Liberty; and yet we have not forfeited our claim to be regarded as a Christian nation. A succession of pure and good men has not been wanting in high places of official power. They have sometimes lifted ineffectual voices on the side of feeble minorities, yet they have, sooner or later, carried their points, for one good man, in a moral contest, having God on his side, is in the majority.

This being a republic, in which the people rule, the temporary elevation of this or that politician to place and power stamps no permanent moral or intellectual character upon the nation. The people—the vast masses in private life—the population away from the hollowness, the corruption, the vices of cities, who live in the free, pure, and beautiful country, give us our character as a Christian nation. The cities all have good men more than sufficient to save them from Sodom's unhappy fate; but to find a place where majorities are on the side of God and of truth, we must go among the agricultural population, where men live in the midst of God's creation—

"Far from the noisy world's ignoble strife."

Were great cities like New York the exponents of our national character, our Government and institutions, with all their excellence, with all their happy realities and auspicious hopes, would long since have been swept away. Ignorance and ruffianism among the lower orders, mammon and licentiousness among the higher circles, would have sealed the ruin of our commercial metropolis, had not its destinies been firmly linked to those of the great, the intelligent, the moral Empire State. The healthy blood which rejuvenates the moral and commercial enterprise of the great cities comes from the country. The sons of farmers and mechanics, who have been reared in rural homes to virtuous and industrious habits, become the political and commercial leaders of the nation.

While we remain an agricultural people, and the majority of the people are brought in constant and immediate contact with God, in the country which He created, we shall retain our right to be known as a Christian nation.

CHAPTER XXVII.

Intemperance—Our Unprofitable Partnership.

The inhabitants of a certain ancient city once had a most untimely and unwelcome rain. Liquid fire fell from heaven and swept away the devoted town, making of its site a bed in which the Dead Sea has lain near four thousand years.

The liquid fire which threatens a deluge to our land is not brewed in the heavens, nor distilled from the clouds, but is prepared by the wicked subversion of the gifts of nature from their proper uses, and the prostitution of their life-preserving properties to the work of death.

Men of perverse minds and misdirected talents have given themselves to the manufacture and sale of intoxicating liquors, and, strange to say, have found the fiery flood of ruin to the land the high tide of fortune to themselves.

Making a plea of restraining the traffic, under such circumstances as make it seem like a desire to participate in the profits of the trade, the body politic has made a partnership with it.

For a stipulated sum the Government lends its countenance and protection to the traffic, thus forming a "league with hell and a covenant with Death."

This partnership has been of no profit to the state. The pittance which has gone into the public treasury from the sale of licenses has been poor compensation for the wretchedness, the poverty, the death, which have fallen like a devouring plague upon the people.

The revenue from licenses is not enough to keep in repair the machinery for the support of pauperism. In some of the states the money received for the sale of liquor licenses goes into the common-school fund and is applied to educational purposes. This pious use of ill-gotten gains makes as poor amends for the iniquitous transaction as did the purchase of the Potter's field, with Judas Iscariot's thirty pieces of silver, for the bargain and sale of the Divine Redeemer.

Consigning a portion of her children to poverty and death, that another numerically insignificant proportion of her progeny may live in palaces and fare sumptuously, is an exhibition of maternal weakness and partiality which makes a serious impeachment against the judgment of our mother country.

The nation should listen to the sepulchral voices coming from the two million drunkards' graves which have been digged and filled in the United States in the last half century. "Hark! from the Tombs" would be "a doleful sound," calculated, if heard aright, to lead the nation to salutary reflection, profound repentance, and happy reformation.

The evil genius which induced the infatuated Jews to cast their offspring into the fire, as a sacrifice to Moloch, has fallen in these latter days upon the American nation. She has cast multitudes of her sons and daughters to feed the fires of intemperance. Many who have not yet perished in the flames are going about with the fatal fires kindled in their vitals.

Post-mortem examinations of persons who have died from intemperance have revealed the fact that their blood has become so fully charged with alcohol that it burns like oil. Examples are not wanting of persons who have indulged in alcoholic drinks so long, that, the blood becoming fully infused with inflammatory ingredient, they have taken fire, and perished by spontaneous combustion.

If individual citizens, who form the vitalizing atoms of the body politic, should generally become infused with the spirituous elements, an accidental spark of excitement might create an explosion which would rend the national framework to atoms, and sacrifice it as a burnt-offering on the altar of sin.

The great work of curing the nation of the disease of intemperance was begun in 1836 by a few resolute men, who commenced the work of national reform in their own private characters. Having been inebriates, who had wasted wealth and health in devotion to strong drink, they knew the dire evils of intemperance, and resolved to break effectually and forever the chains of evil habit. They formed the Washingtonian Society, and pledged themselves to abstain from everything that would intoxicate. They applied themselves with energy to the work of spreading the principles of total abstinence, and organizing temperance societies. Within a few years their efforts were crowned with marked and salutary effect upon the nation.

In 1851 the note of progress sounded still louder, and the friends of reform resolved to make a more decided advance. Legal protection and partnership was a stronghold in which the liquor traffic had intrenched itself. It was resolved to drive its mercenaries from behind their intrenchments, and turn their guns against themselves. A determined effort was made to enlist law on the side of Temperance Reform. The movement was begun in our frontier Northeastern state. Other portions of the country followed her example, and soon not less than twelve states had enacted stringent laws against the importation and sale of intoxicating liquors.

In 1856 the enemies of reform gained a temporary victory in Maine, and expunged the prohibitory law from the statute-book; but the friends of progress rallied their forces, and hurled the votaries of intemperance from power.

In some other states, where similar enactments had been made, the judicial ermine was tainted with corruption, and the law, fraught with blessings for present and succeeding generations, was declared "unconstitutional." "Liquor" was again allowed to inundate lands from which it had been restrained by legal barrier.

Men whose names are appended to such decisions will take rank among the infamous judges who have cursed mankind by their wicked and ill-advised "opinions." Most unhappy is a nation which is cursed by such mischievous men at the fountain-head of justice. In years to come, when civilization and Christianity shall exercise their benign influence over the hearts and minds of a majority of the human race, their names will only be remembered for the evil that they have done. If they have done mischief for renown, like the infamous incendiary who fired the Temple of Diana at Ephesus, they may realize the unenviable fame they seek, and have their names spoken with curses in centuries to come.

The armies of slavery having been vanquished on the field of battle, the weapons of warfare should now be turned against intemperance, another "relic of barbarism." The soldiers of Reform, flushed with victory gained on other fields, may now turn their arms against this great national evil, with prospect of success.

CHAPTER XXVIII.

Our Fountain of Youth—How the Nation Renews Her Strength.

The substance of the human body is continually changing. Old particles pass off and new substance is deposited, so that in course of seven years we inhabit new bodies. Unseen and silently the busy atoms come and go. Like the coral insect, which conducts its small and mighty labors in the bosom of the sea, their deeds are only divulged in their effects. The elastic step of youth retained through many years, the hand ever strong and skillful to perform the nicest requirements of the mind, the eye losing not its radiance until death comes with violent hand to put out the light of life—all show how careful are the lively atoms to relieve one another, and how readily they come up, each with its own freshness and vigor, to bear a part in the physical labors of life.

Similar changes take place in the body politic. Old and worn-out particles are removed, while new and vigorous units come in to supply the loss. In course of thirty years the whole substance of the state is changed, yet the constitution and national identity remain.

It is a wise providential arrangement in national affairs, that when a man has acted his part and can be no longer useful to the state, a lymphatic is at hand to absorb him as waste and worn-out matter. He glides away on the Lethean stream which bears on its bosom all the past.

If by this arrangement a state loses the services of the good and wise, there is compensation in the fact that it is the process by which the patient people have always been relieved, sooner or later, of wicked tyrants and designing demagogues. Thus poor Naples, a few years since, in the course of nature, was relieved of her loathsome and ungodly "King Bomba." Any successor attempting to walk in his footsteps would require many years to compass all his crimes and descend to the same depths of political and personal transgression.

If new and healthful matter is not deposited as dead substance is removed, the body politic becomes emaciated, loses its vigor, and soon dies. In America the reinforcement has always been greater than the loss; hence the Republic has enjoyed a healthy and vigorous growth. As old statesmen and gray-haired citizens pass away, youth arrive at manhood and hasten forward to occupy the vacant places. Vitalized with new and energetic life, they come to prolong the vigor of the state. Patriotic citizens die, and the voices of great statesmen are hushed in the silence of the grave, yet the state knows no decline in wisdom nor in power.

It is of vital importance that the fresh particles of matter which enter into the frame-work of the body should be freighted with no insidious disease. Melancholy would be our fate should malady and death enter by the avenues open to admit the messengers of life and health. Unhappy would be our case if the reinforcing atoms, glowing with the hues of apparent health and happiness, should prove to be tinged with the baleful color of contagion and disease.

Such would be our desperate condition should the youth of America become evil-minded and corrupt. Every such atom added to the body politic would only augment the mass of corruption and disease.

When Catiline resolved upon the subversion of the Roman Republic, he commenced his work by attempting to corrupt the youth. By all means within his reach he infused the virus of immorality into their hearts and lives. By every manner of ingenious device he pandered to their baser passions. He sowed the seeds of anarchy and ruin to the state in the susceptible soil of youthful hearts, and it was only by the stupendous labors of Cicero and the patriotic people that the republic was able to defer, for a season, the labor of gathering the dreadful harvest of desolation.

Happily the American Republic can as yet see no source of fear in the promise of her youthful sons and daughters. With a few exceptions, such as will always appear while human nature wears its present form, there exists in American youth an amiable willingness to be taught, and a readiness to walk in paths of wisdom.

As aged and experienced laborers grow weary in their country's service, and rest from their toils, recruits from the ranks of virtuous youth advance, with fresh and vigorous powers, to take in their hands the implements of honest industry. No lull in the hum of manufactures, no cessation in the bustle of commerce, marks the interval between successive generations.

The American nation rejoices in a career of constant progress. Each generation adds its cumulative energies to those which achieved the successes of the past. Each age is endowed with more muscle to accomplish the physical labors of the time, and with more mind to push further the domain of thought.

The American nation never need arrive at dotage or decline. She has discovered means for the renewal and augmentation of her youthful energies more effectual than the fabled Fountain of Youth, which charmed with fallacious hope the adventurous spirits of Spanish cavaliers.

Ponce de Leon had grown old in the military service of the Spanish Crown when Columbus returned from that first grand voyage which revealed to Europe the existence of a new Western World. His spirit glowed with desire for adventures in a new and more romantic field. Advancing age might have deterred him from undertaking the toils and perils attending a voyage of discovery and conquest to the Western wilderness, had not his mind been infused with the pleasing fancy that there existed, somewhere amid the green and flowery recesses of the West, a fountain which had the miraculous virtue of restoring the vigor and vivacity of youth to all so fortunate as to drink of its pellucid and ever-flowing waters. Ponce de Leon and other cavaliers of similar adventurous spirit landed on the shores of Florida and penetrated the flowery forests, but sought in vain to find that fountain from which should flow the elixir of life. Ponce de Leon and most of his cavaliers fell victims to the arrows of the Indians, the hardships of the march, and the diseases of the clime. A few returned to Europe, only to yield at last to that inevitable death which no earthly power could avert.

The American Republic has discovered a Fountain of Youth more magical in its effects upon herself than would have been the waters sought so ardently and vainly by Spanish cavaliers. This fountain flows for her benefit alone, since it has no virtue for the renewal of individual life. Its waters flow from a million happy American homes, whence virtuous youth go forth to take useful stations in the land.

This fountain springs not most purely amid the stone-paved streets and narrow lanes of crowded cities. It gushes most brightly and most copiously amid the hills and valleys of the grand and quiet country.

Cities abound in great sins and resistless temptations, which sweep away and swallow up the greater portion of the youth. Their loss to themselves and their friends is irreparable, but to the nation it is more than made up by the virtuous and vigorous contributions of the country. The youth of rural origin are those who rise to the highest places in the land. Away from crowded cities, in the rural districts, there are less temptation, more habits of industry early learned, higher appreciation of the fewer educational advantages, and more deference to the authority of parents and teachers. Thus the fountain of mental and moral health is kept pure, and flows perpetually for the nation's benefit.

Amid the crowded populations of great cities, fathers are so filled with speculations to make fortunes, or labors to make livelihoods, and mothers so occupied with society, that they devote but little time to the mental and moral interests of their children, who are permitted to grow up amid unlimited indulgence and unmitigated idleness.

The sons and daughters of the country are taught to bear their part and proportion in domestic and farm labors. Division of labors and duties among the members of the household gives to all some hours of leisure, which may be devoted to domestic society, education, and religion.

The fountain of health and youthful vigor to the nation gushes forth in perennial brightness from free schools and Sunday-schools, which spread their genial influence over every hillside and valley of the land.

He who poisons the wells and springs at which the unsuspecting population drink, is not only a murderer, but a monster. A fountain designed to promote the nation's health and strength gushes on the banks of the Hudson. So precious did its waters appear, that the nation devoted large sums to promote its enlargement and secure its purity. It was collected in marble basins and flowed over golden sands. A stealthy foe crept in, and, "while men slept," cast poison into the pellucid waters. Its effect was not immediately visible; the waters flowed apparently as pure as ever. In an hour of emergency, when the nation needed extraordinary vigor to meet a great crisis in her history, she turned to her favorite fountain, and would have drunk a fatal draught, had not her quick eye discovered that it was "casting up mire and dirt." With disgust she turned to the native springs which gush from the mountains of New England and the hill-sides of the West.

By constant contributions from her well-ordered families and schools, the body politic maintains its health and grows in strength. The nation asks of fathers and mothers the devotion of their children to her service. It is not demanded that all shall become statesmen and politicians. The great majority may be more useful to the state in other fields of labor.

The devotement which the nation asks is not a sacrifice such as Pagan Moloch demanded of his idolatrous worshipers. The children are not to be cast into the fire or be slain upon the altar. The Republic asks that they shall live and labor for their own highest interests, and in doing this they promote in the best manner the advancement of the nation.

Ancient mythology says that Saturn was addicted to an unparental habit of devouring his children as soon as they were born. Had not the mother, by a pardonable fraud, deceived the voracious and unnatural father, little Jupiter would have gone the way of his elder-born brothers and sisters, and epitomized all the acts of his life in ministering a meal to the parental stomach, instead of hurling thunderbolts from Mount Olympus, and doing other marvelous deeds.

The American nation does not devour her children for her own personal gratification and their destruction. While she would have them contribute to her growth and strength, she desires that they shall retain their own identity, and long live to promote their own greatest personal good. It is the policy of a despotism to crush out the lives and hopes of the people, and consolidate them in one great mass, whose only use is to increase the momentum of irresponsible power.

Sempronia, the Roman matron, with just maternal pride, esteemed her children as her choicest jewelry. The nation numbers her studious, intelligent, and virtuous youth among her brightest jewels.

Foreign nations, who keep those expensive and useless pieces of ornamental furniture styled kings and queens, possess certain senseless baubles which they call "crown jewels."

The children of America are the jewels which sparkle in her coronet, and manifest her true and royal sovereignty. They are her chief pledges of the power she wields and the dignity she enjoys. They declare that when other nations, now enjoying an ephemeral power, have had their day and disappeared from the stage of national affairs, America will have only entered upon her heritage of perpetually-renewing youthfulness.

CHAPTER XXIX.

Nations are not Immortal, and States do Sometimes Die.

Death is recognized in all the world as a crowned and sceptered king. None dispute his sway; none successfully resist his authority. The people fall obediently before him, and kings yield in silence to his decrees.

Death has walked abroad without hinderance or restriction during all the past. Everywhere he has crushed beneath his feet the delicate organism of life. He has rudely shaken to the ground and trampled in the dust the leaves of verdure and beauty which have adorned the world. Death has strewn the trophies of his triumphs so thickly that scarcely any portion of the earth's crust has not passed through his destroying hand.

While myriads of living things have passed away, leaving no trace of their existence, a few have left memorials of their lives. Some have written their autobiographies with footprints in the rocks. Although these are all the traces of existence which many extinct animals have left in the archives of nature, yet the skillful geologist has been able, even in these faint records, to read accurate descriptions of their habits, and reproduce their portraits.

The hardness of the frame-work of some animals is the means by which they have held out against decay, and obtained recognition and reputation in times long subsequent to the termination of their lives. Their shells or bones, imbedded in the rock, have been exhumed, and are preserved as specimens in the cabinets of the curious.

The dead of the human race greatly outnumber the living. The remains of man are thickly strewn throughout the formation which has been rising during the period of his existence.

The Chinese have sought to add to their overweening self-esteem and meager reputation by constructing for themselves chronologies reaching many thousands of years anterior to the remotest date of authentic human history. The records of geology put the stamp of falsehood upon all such foolish pretensions. They clearly show that man's origin dates back but six thousand years. Only in deposits made within this time, known as the historic or human period, are found the remains of man. A few undistinguished bones exhumed from soil favorable to their preservation, and some nameless mummies stored in catacombs, afford the only evidence of former bodily existence furnished by the countless and forgotten multitudes of ancient centuries.

Death is likewise the lot of nations. Relics of former national existence are seen in the remains of laws and constitutions to be found in fragmentary form in the politics of existing nations; as the broken columns which once supported the magnificent temples of antiquity furnish materials to the modern inhabitants of classical countries for the construction of their cottages. Traces of the national life of ancient Rome may be seen in portions of the jurisprudence of modern nations borrowed from the "Twelve Tables" and the Justinian Code.

Many of the elder nations were rude in their manners and modes of government. Bent upon their rough pleasures and unproductive pursuits, they left to their successors the labor of taming the wilderness and building the institutions of civilization. Ancient nations, however, were not all so low in the scale of excellence as to cause the recital of their history and condition to appear flattery of present times. Some of them reached such elevation in literature and government as to cause the story of their attainments to seem more like satire on modern nations than unvarnished historic truth. Many of their works excite the emulation, and shame the achievements of modern times.

The greatest and most beautiful monuments of those polished nations are their literary works. Multiplied by the modern printing-press, they have become imperishable. They are the beautiful windows through which we may see the genius which adorned the olden times. We are thus brought into immediate contact with minds which gave ornament and reputation to the greatest nations of antiquity.

With individuals, death is a natural event, which no one hopes to shun. All expect, in some coming time, to open the doors of the soul's frail tabernacle to admit the fatal guest. It requires no long course of observation on the human race to arrive at a knowledge of the universal reign of death.

A man of speculative mind may sometimes amuse himself with constructing and carrying to its consequences a theory that men do not die. He proceeds to draw therefrom most beautiful and glowing inferences. Under the hypothesis that death is excluded from human society, he fancies happiness is greatly augmented, and the progress of the race promoted.

"How much less pain!" he says; "what utter inexperience of bereavement! what a happy exemption from physicians' fees and undertakers' bills!"

Your theory sounds well; but, unfortunately, my kind friend, it has an existence only in your glowing imagination. All your fine-drawn deductions do not obviate the ghastly fact that men die. Facts constantly occurring prove beyond controversy that mortality is still the common lot.

"Hold," says the theorist; "see to what unhappy consequences your principle must lead. It tends inevitably to the dissolution and extinction of families and even nations."

Can't help it, sir. It will not mend matters to ignore self-evident facts.

"Whatever may be the import of your facts, I am resolved to prevent, if possible, the extinction of my family, by rejecting the theory that death is a necessary and inevitable event. If, by accident or disease, any of my family should be reduced to a coldness and a pallor in any way resembling what has been commonly called death, they shall retain their places in the family, and be treated in all respects as before."

You will find, my friend, that dead bodies, bolstered in their places for the purpose of keeping up a family organization, will rather have the opposite, the disintegrating effect, and would better be recognized in their true relations at once.

The theory of ignoring death as an inevitable event in personal history, being so manifestly groundless and absurd, it seems strange that a similar error should have crept into the politics of certain statesmen.

"It is impossible for a state to secede," they say. "No state can commit suicide, and die a political death."

"How do you substantiate your beautiful theory?" asks an incredulous querist.

"The Constitution knows nothing of secession, for this would be to provide for its own destruction. Secession is a great moral wrong, since it unjustly deprives multitudes of innocent people of their dearest heritage of rights."

Secession is indeed a crime against the Constitution and against moral law—a principle in ethics which has only very recently found its way into the philosophy of some ardent theorists; and yet such an admission does not rule it out of existence. There are many flagrant sins against human and divine law, whose existence is too evident to admit of doubt.

Murder is a great crime against human society, and suicide is sinful, yet both do sometimes occur.

"To allow the principle that states may die, is to introduce a disintegrating element into the Government. Allow this doctrine, and the Union becomes no better than a rope of sand."

No, it is not the admission of the existence of crime that shall endanger the existence of the Union, but to blind our eyes to the fact that crime exists, to call it by another name, to fail to follow it with punishment proportioned to the offense—these must tend to destroy the Federal Government.

The Southern States are guilty of the last great crime against human nature and human law. They committed an offense which absorbs and swallows up all others, as the ocean swallows up the waters of all streams. These hapless states should not be denied the wages due their deeds—wages which, as footed up in the great Ledger of Divinity, are denominated "death."

It were a solemn mockery to treat dead states as if they were alive; to seat them in the places where they were wont to perform their acts of sovereignty in former years, and cause them to make some muscular movements, by means of federal galvanism or machinery, and call it life.

Better be rid of this burdensome ceremony at once; bury the old, inanimate forms out of sight, and allow new and better systems to occupy the vacant places.

There is no national limit to the life of states, and no inherent necessity that they should ever die. They are allowed to live during good behavior. Their careers are coextensive with their virtue. No nation ever perished, in all the past, that did not fall a victim to its own crimes.

The old and charitable proverb, *Nil de mortuis nisi bonum*, advises us to say nothing concerning the dead save what is good. The knowledge that we shall all erelong pass beyond the possibility of refuting slanders and apologizing for errors, makes us willing to throw the mantle of charity over the frailties of the dead. If we can not praise, we are at liberty to maintain a charitable silence.

This Latin proverb has not the force of law in favor of dead nations. The presumption is all against the decedents. The statement that a nation no longer exists is a grave charge against it. The imagination, if not the memory, calls up the career of sin, the solemn arraignment, the just sentence, the condign punishment.

Human history is a book of precedents, wherein are recorded the high crimes for which nations have been consigned to punishment. Herein the high courts which investigate the crimes of nations will never lack the support which precedents give to judicial acts. Nations can not fail to receive abundant admonition of the miserable fate which shall overtake them in a career of transgression.

Many nations have had their origin in crime. Evil was implanted in their constitutions, and had its outgrowth in the miserable lives of the wretched people. Crime, with them, was allowed every facility for free and full development.

The besetting sin of many nations has been ambition. Fired with zeal for conquest, they have gone forth to foreign war. By virtue of the energy and activity inspired by their ruling passion, they have had longer lives, and occupied more conspicuous places in history, than those ignoble races which have submitted themselves as slaves to avarice, and have fallen victims to the luxury and sloth always attendant upon ill-gotten wealth. All alike have been consigned to the tomb where lie in their eternal sleep all wicked nations, whose crimes have had time to culminate and produce legitimate effects.

Sin, of whatsoever kind, and how small soever its beginning, gathers force and fury as it proceeds, and finally overwhelms the unhappy author of its existence.

The builders of a state should look well to what they do, and overlook no blemish, however small, in human character. A very small offense has time for unlimited enlargement in the long career which is set before a state. The builders of a political fabric should beware, lest in the very foundation-stones there may be some element of disintegration which at last shall cause the massive walls to crumble.

The most practical way to prolong our national existence is not in rending the air with frantic huzzas for the "glorious Union." No government has ever been so evil, or so near its doom, that some have not been found to asseverate its excellence, and set forth the infinite importance of its perpetuation. Such declamation has never delayed for a moment the fall of the sword of justice suspended over the heads of national transgressors.

The only legitimate and successful way of prolonging a nation's life is, with honest hand and steady purpose to eradicate evil of every hue and shape.

Thousands of true saviors of their country are dwelling, unknown to fame, in our populous cities and in our rural districts. They inhabit mansions of wealth, and dwell in rude cabins on the far frontier. They sometimes find their ways to places of power in the Capital, but more frequently their deeds of patriotic statesmanship are performed at home. They are those who labor to improve their own personal characters by removing evil and engrafting good. They are those whose voices and votes are steadily given for the removal of private and public sins.

Radical reforms, beginning in private life, and working upward into national character, are the renovating and rejuvenating processes of the body politic. Virtues springing up from the depths of individual hearts, and flowering in the deeds of private citizens, produce the fruit of that tree of life, of which the nation may eat, and live while time endures.

CHAPTER XXX.

THE PARADISE OF NATIONS AND THE POLITICAL LIFE TO COME.

THE heaven which charms the fancy of the Oriental dreamer is a paradise of sensual delights, where elevated aims and sober duties are unknown, where the inhabitants enjoy an existence of voluptuous ease.

The Indian's heaven is a happy hunting-ground, where the red man shall enjoy constant and unalloyed indulgence in the pleasures and excitements of the chase.

The Christian's Heaven is a happy state and glorious place, where the pious soul and spiritual body, eliminated of all earthly grossness, shall dwell forever in the presence of God.

There is destined to be a heaven upon earth, into which shall be admitted all good nations which prolong their lives by a career of virtue and a course of self-correction, from which all nations incorrigibly bad shall be excluded by their previous deaths.

Many people believe that the earth, refined and purified by the fires of the last day, shall form a part of the "new heavens and the new earth."

The Paradise of Nations shall be fitted up before the day of Divine judgment. The globe will probably retain many of its present features, but they will be animated and spiritualized by a higher virtue and a brighter intelligence. The whole sphere of earth shall be the seat of that grand paradise, and the whole race of man shall be gathered under its starry canopy.

Many political systems, once greatly admired, shall not pass through the ordeal of ages intervening, and shall never have admittance to the glorious futurity to which they have aspired. Some forms of government and national constitutions now existing shall be found then, but so greatly changed and so much improved as to be scarcely recognized by their projectors.

As a prerequisite to admission to the Paradise of Nations, there must be vitality enough to exist until the date of its inauguration. As the first element of vitality in a government is virtue, no nation destitute of correct principles can hope to be found among those highly favored and happy peoples.

God designs that all the inhabitants of earth in the last ages shall be happy, hence no form of government which does not subserve man's highest interests shall survive until that time. By this principle all despotic and aristocratic governments will be excluded.

Great Britain may hope to have a place in the paradise of the great and happy future, but in a form so changed as to bear but faint resemblance to her former self. Her present people would scarcely recognize the new and highly exalted state.

Long previous to the happy era here described, she has denied herself the expensive indulgence of a "royal family." She no longer sits under the shade of hereditary sovereignty. Men who are voted by the people to have integrity and talent to transact national affairs are given due credit for what they do, and are not required to stand behind a man of straw, denominated "Britannic Majesty."

The English have made the discovery that the first-born son is no better than his brothers, and is not entitled, by "accident of birth," to the exclusive enjoyment of all wealth and honors which his parents have possessed.

With the repeal of all laws of primogeniture, the key-stone of the arch of aristocracy has fallen, and the whole architecture has crumbled away and mingled with common dust. The multiplied square miles of English soil which so long were kept a "howling wilderness," to furnish hunting-grounds for noblemen, have been divided and subdivided into fruitful gardens. The children of great landed proprietors have forgotten their noble ancestry, having long before been swallowed up in the undistinguished mass.

Ireland, whose complaints became so chronic that Carlyle declared that the only adequate remedy for the ills of the island would be its submergence in the sea for twenty-four hours, has been purified without such hydropathy, and has been elevated without such emergence from the sea, and now stands, side by side, a sister state with England in the Republic of Great Britain.

India long since served through the years of her apprenticeship to England, and stands forth a free, independent, Christian Republic.

The French Empire has no existence. It went down with the infidelity and licentiousness of the race upon whose degradation it was built.

The Republic of Switzerland, having overleaped its Alpine boundaries, has formed the nucleus of a democracy which extends from the Atlantic to the eastern confines of the old and extinct Empire of Austria.

Russia, which entered the path of progress under Peter the Great, having made great forward strides, in the nineteenth century, by giving freedom to the serfs, has ever since made constant and steady progress. Poland and Hungary, once so deeply wronged by her, now form sovereign and independent members of her united states. Siberia is a part of the Russian Republic, no longer used as the abode and burial-place of unhappy exiles. It is dotted with smiling villages and cheerful homes, which rob the wintery clime of half of its gloom.

China, whose exclusive domain was first pierced by railroads and telegraphs near the end of the nineteenth century, having adopted all the improvements of other nations, now takes such liberal views of all the outside world, that the eyes of her children no longer grow obliquely in their heads. The Chinese man of fashion has cut off his queue, and wears his hair as other men. Female feet are allowed to grow to normal size, and the human understanding among that once narrow-minded people has attained to considerable enlargement.

The Republic of United Africa has become a favorite abode of enlightenment and freedom. Civilization, which, in the early history of the world, had its first and highest development in

Egypt, having gone forth to illuminate the other continents, has returned to its former home, and now illuminates all Africa. The end of that mysterious providence, by which the unhappy children of Africa were dragged away westward into bondage, now appears in the results which fill the continent to overflowing with American language, literature, and politics. The wrath of man has signally wrought the praise of God.

The United States of America is the acknowledged leader and exemplar of nations. Being first among nations to enjoy the blessings of liberty, she has communicated lessons of freedom to mankind, who have grown to regard her with the deference due a teacher. Her domain has so greatly enlarged that the ocean has become her boundary on every hand. This extension has not resulted from military conquest. American philanthropy would not allow indigent and unhappy nations knocking at her gates to be debarred admission to the Republic, since to share the blessings of liberty is to increase the common stock.

Canada, having grown weary of an impracticable confederation of provinces unnecessarily subordinate to a transatlantic power, now forms a happy and prosperous portion of the American Union. Mexico is freed from foreign rulers and domestic discords. She has closed her long chapter of political troubles, by subscribing to the American Constitution, and contributing her entire family of twenty-three states to the Federal Union.

The old Southern states have become loyal and prosperous. Their genial climate and fertile soil, occupied and cultivated by a free and happy people, render them the most attractive portion of the globe. Long after the failure of their unhappy attempt at rebellion, they cherished a foolish hostility toward the Northern states and the innocent victims of their rapacity, their emancipated slaves. This obstruction long impeded the progress of the South. It prevented the southward flow of capital and industry, and proved almost as great a blight as the original curse of slavery. The foolish prejudice against inhabitants of other latitudes at length wholly passed away, having received its death-blow in the downfall of slavery.

Nowhere throughout the world is a fair skin considered a necessary qualification for a citizen. Wealth is no longer an indispensable passport to honor and distinction.

The Constitution has been amended and improved, until it is as nearly perfect as any human work can be. Recognizing God as the Supreme Ruler of nations and individuals, it is next in sacredness and binding force to the Holy Word. The Constitution guarantees equal rights to all, and gives exclusive privileges to none. The powers of the different departments of the Government are so accurately and nicely determined, that the people have the utmost security against the disintegration of the Government and the establishment of tyranny.

Presidents are chosen not with reference to the locality of their homes, or the strength of their influence to cause men to drill according to the forms of party tactics. They are men whose dignity and elevated personal character are consonant with the high office which they hold. They are distinguished, not by their volubility in popular harangue, but by the wisdom and statesmanship of the plans by which they secure the harmony and prosperity of the country. Since, in the progress of the Constitution toward perfection, the provision by which the President is eligible for re-election has been stricken out, all temptation to employ power and patronage, simply to secure a second term of office, has been removed, and the Executive mind is free to devote its energies to the achievement of an administration which shall well compare with the most prosperous which have gone before.

Members of Congress do not owe their election to their facility in making stump-speeches, and their skill in working the wires of local politics, but rather to their profound insight into the principles upon which republican government is based, and their ability to rise above the prejudice which limits narrow minds to the selfish interests of a small constituency.

Voters can all read their ballots, and have sufficient skill in the use of the pen to draw lines of erasure across the names of candidates whose principles are not accordant with their own. They allow themselves no longer to be whipped into the traces of party by those who hold the reins and wield the lash. They no longer bend their shoulders to drag the triumphal chariots of demagogues through the mire into which evil practices have plunged them.

Christian people are not afraid to take an interest and a part in politics, lest their garments should be defiled in the "muddy pool." No pharisaical spirit now induces them to stand aloof, and say, "I would rather risk being lost in a ship managed by incompetent sailors, than to pollute my hands by working the greasy ropes." Politics and law afford as appropriate fields for the activity of the Christian as any other department of life and labor.

Christian sects, which once divided their energies and weakened their influence by their disagreements with one another, have long ago made such a harmonious and combined attack upon the strongholds of error, that these have been carried by assault; and Satan, driven to unfrequented dens and caves, to which he once pursued the persecuted saints, is meditating a final abandonment of the mundane sphere. Religious denominations in every land are all happily separated from legal wedlock with the state, and consequently exercise a most potent and salutary influence upon the government of the world.

Ministers of the Gospel are no longer decried for denouncing political sins.

Statesmen find the Scriptures a rich treasury of political wisdom. They have not only heard of the Bible, but have diligently studied its principles, and seldom misquote or misapply the sacred Word. They no longer use the words of Scripture as "glittering generalities," to round a rhetorical flourish, but as their practical rule of faith and practice.

Lawyers labor not to pervert the ends of justice, or darken counsel by words without wisdom. Their occupation is not gone, although the majority of men are no longer rogues. They find employment in oiling the bearings of the legal machinery, so that the wheels of justice run noiselessly, swiftly, and certainly toward their destination.

Physicians have cast aside all systems and nostrums which tend to undermine the constitution, rather than to lengthen human life. They are accredited officers of health, and receive compensation for the time their patients are well, rather than for the number of days in which they are sick. Since each day's sickness diminishes the physician's fee, his anxious care and chief concern is given to make men well and keep them so.

Mechanics, being the bone and sinew, the health and strength of the nation, are held in merited esteem by those who derive luxuries and comforts from their hard-handed toil. By their progress in intelligence and skill, and the multiplied improvements in labor-saving contrivances, they secure a competent support by less hours of labor, and the leisure thus secured they devote to the cultivation of their minds and the education of their families.

Farmers have wrought so intelligently upon the surface of the earth, that they have brought it well-nigh back to Eden-like loveliness. They have transformed the primal curse of labor into a blessing. They have allowed thorns and briers to spring up so rarely, that evidence scarcely can be found that earth was ever cursed for human sin.

Merchants are content with reasonable gains, and are not in such haste to grow rich as to rush headlong into bankruptcy. There is no longer arrayed against them the prejudice which existed in the days of monkish intolerance, causing to be enacted the illiberal canon: "*Homo Mercator vix aut nunquam potest Deo placere*," etc. "A merchant can scarcely, if at all, please God, and, therefore, no Christian should be a merchant, and if he wishes to be one, let him be expelled the Church of God." Being governed in all his transactions by the principles of Christianity, the man of trade and commerce has become the practical missionary of the Gospel, and the peacemaker of world.

Railroads, overlying the continents, form enduring bands of interest and friendship, which unite far-separated people. Telegraphs permeating every sea, and interlacing every land, do much to prevent or correct misunderstandings, and render wars unnecessary.

Moral and intellectual elements in national

character have grown to such preponderance, that nations do not resort to violence for the adjustment of grievances. They have organized a grand Representative Assembly, whose acts are final in all matters relating to international law.

The world moves in harmony with the Universe. The terrestrial sphere, revolving about the sun, forms part of the solar system, which moves as a portion of the grand "frame of the Universe" about the Throne of God.

The political system is no less harmonious and complete. Intelligent and moral people constitute the population of the states which combine to make the republics, whose domains constitute the political and physical sphere of earth.

The republics which possess the world form the well-regulated "Family of Nations," which lives and moves in orderly obedience to the Universal Father.

THE END.

www.ingramcontent.com/pod-product-compliance
Lightning Source LLC
Chambersburg PA
CBHW030813230426
43667CB00008B/1191